rown Babies, Pink Parents is a real world guide for White
rents who are raising Black children. Author Amy Ford is the adoptive mother
three African American daughters, with first-hand experience of the chal-
ges of transracial parenting. She addresses a multitude of concerns including
sic skin and hair care, racial socialization, accepting white privilege, and ways to
lebrate the diversity of your family.

BROWN BABIES, PINK PARENTS

"A humor... ... ...
multi cu...

Amy Ford lives in Austin, TX with
her partner, Kim, and their three
daughters. As a foster parent since
2002, Amy has parented numerous
children, most of whom are African
American. She now serves as the
Director for Parenting Across Color,
a non-profit organization dedicated
to educating and supporting the
white parents of black children.

Amy Ford

"Amy has learned so very much from her
experiences and shares them in a very open,
conversational tone with the reader."

- RUTH G. MCROY DAVIS, PH.D.,
RESEARCH PROFESSOR, UNIVERSITY OF TEXAS AT AUSTIN SCHOOL OF SOCIAL WORK

# Brown Babies
# Pink Parents

NY BOOKS HAVE BEEN WRITTEN ABOUT
NSRACIAL ADOPTION FOR FAMILIES, BUT
S ONE PROVIDES THE PRACTICAL 'HOW-TO'S"

ISBN 978-0-557-53932-1
90000

9 780557 539321

FOREWORD BY
DR. RUTH G. MCROY DAVIS

BY Amy Ford

A PRACTICAL GUIDE TO TRANSRACIAL PARENTING

hotos courtesy of Tricia Boudreaux, Amy Ford, and Tanya Gleixner; back photograph courtesy of Laurie Boecker, Captured Photo Studio; cover design by Karen Barry

# Brown Babies
# Pink Parents

# Brown Babies
# Pink Parents

## Amy Ford

Triple M Productions
Austin, Texas

Book and cover design and production by Karen Barry

Copyediting by M. Jane Ross, MJR Publishing Services, Austin, TX, mjr@io.com

Front cover photographs by Amy Ford, Tricia Boudreaux, and Tanya Gleinser. Used with permission of the photographers.

Back cover photo © 2010 by Laurie Boecker, Captured Photo Studio, Austin, TX


Manufactured in the United States of America

Softcover ISBN 978-0-557-53932-1

The following articles and excerpts are reprinted with permission of the author except as noted:

In chapter 3, the article, "Seven Common Transracial Parenting Mistakes," by Willie B. Garrett.

In chapter 7, the article, "A Transracially Adopted Child's Bill of Rights." Reprinted with the permission of Pact: An Adoption Alliance.

In chapter 8, the list "Top 11 Critical Tools Needed to Style a Child's Hair."

See the endnotes for bibliographic information on sources.

*This book is lovingly dedicated to all my girls,*
*Madison, McKenzie, Morgan and Kim*

# Table of Contents

# Foreword

According to the most recent data available, 30% of the 123,000 children needing adoption in the US are African-American (AFCARS, 2008).[1] Growing numbers of white families are fostering and adopting these children. However, as Amy Ford in this wonderful book notes, "Love is *not* enough," when trying to be a successful transracial adoptive family. In a world in which race matters, Amy notes that knowledge is needed to better prepare families for the many unforeseen experiences in parenting transracially. This book provides excellent real world insights into transracial parenting and is written in such a down-to-earth manner that families of all backgrounds will learn something — about privilege, race, prejudice, identity, and just being a nurturing parent. Love and admiration for the three little girls whom the author and her partner, Kim, adopted is so clearly evident in every sentence of this book. It's a how-to book for white parents who have adopted African-American children. Amy compares and contrasts her real life awareness and experiences of prejudice and discrimination while growing up in Mississippi to her life now raising three African-American daughters, Madison, McKenzie and Morgan.

I first met Amy and Kim when Ora Ann Houston and I formed the Parenting Across Color (PAC) support group for transracial adopters at St. James Episcopal Church in Austin, Texas. It provided a wonderful opportunity to get to know families who had adopted transracially and to connect them with community resources. After I relocated to Sacramento, California, Amy assumed the leadership of the group and I continue to be so very impressed with the growth in size of PAC and commend Amy for her leadership. Now, Amy has drawn from her personal parenting experiences and her tremendous resourcefulness to develop this wonderful resource book to help and support other families taking this journey.

Although having completed only seven years in the role of a parent, Amy has experienced more than some may have in a lifetime of parenting! It is very clear that Amy has learned so very much about transracial adoptions. Not only has she successfully sought out resources, support groups, neighborhoods, churches, friends, stores, products, beauticians, community events, and vacations that support her transracial family, in this book, she shares how she did it and provides practical tips for other families. Many books have been written about transracial adoption for transracial families, but this one provides the practical how-to's, including even modeling a conversation with a parent and child who had questioned whether her daughter Maddie's family could even be a real one, "since she doesn't have a dad and everyone is a different color." Amy has learned so very much from her experiences and shares them in a very open, conversational tone with the reader.

As Amy notes, she and Kim fostered and adopted three African-American children and they were *not* given any preparation or training for transracial parenting. What she learned, she learned herself, as a result of her commitment to be the best parent possible to her daughters. She acknowledges that adoption is a challenge itself, but transracial adoption brings up new issues and families must be resourceful in trying to meet their cultural, physical, spiritual and emotional needs.

To keep other families from beginning the process of transracial parenting without adequate preparation, Amy has shared her story and those of several other transracial adoptive families in this wonderful collection. Moreover, Amy provides a brief history of transracial adoptions and comprehensively covers the real-life experiences, needs, and questions that many families have but may be hesitant to ask about. Amy talks openly about African-American hair care, how to find products, how to wash hair, and what you need for braids. She gives very practical tips for finding day care, a hairstylist, skin care and more. Cultural traditions such as holidays, African art, food, and literature are all included.

As a real bonus, throughout the book Amy includes resource materials that can be used by families and in training adoption professionals and families. Early in the book she presents a ten item quiz, "Assessing Your Knowledge of African-American Culture," and a ten-item personal inventory for families to assess their readiness for the experience of parenting across the color line. She refers the reader to Peggy McIntosh's highly acclaimed piece on "White Privilege," and includes a reprint of

Willie Garrett's well-known article, "Seven Common Transracial Parenting Mistakes."

I applaud Amy for sharing her family's life story and providing this amazing compendium of practical knowledge about parenting transracially. Thanks so much for this gift to transracial families and children.

*Dr. Ruth G. McRoy Davis*
Research Professor
Ruby Lee Piester Centennial Professor Emerita
Senior Research Fellow, Evan B. Donaldson Adoption Institute
The University of Texas at Austin School of Social Work
Sacramento, California, June 2010

# Preface

I am passionate about my children. I could tell a thousand different stories about the ways my children make me laugh, make me cry, and make me a better person. I worked hard to create this family and I love to tell the story of the way these brown babies stole the heart of this pink parent. It hasn't been an easy journey and what I have learned in the process of raising a child of a different race could fill the state of Texas.

My mother used to remind me regularly that God didn't send an instruction manual when I was born. The same is true for children who are adopted and especially true for transracial adoptions. I was a foster parent for eight years and never received a single hour of training on parenting a child of a different race. I did spend nine weeks learning how to be a foster parent, but during that training, nothing ever came up about race, despite the fact the majority of the foster children who would come into my home were African-American. Foster and adoptive parents need instruction on parenting across the color line. We need a safe place to learn and to make mistakes and to try again. We need to be with other people who understand the struggles we face. How incredibly helpful it would have been to receive the training and support I needed from our agency! Years later I realize there aren't many agencies who do address the deeply personal and highly emotional topic of race.

My partner, Kim, and I have adopted three African-American daughters through foster care. Kim is the youngest of five children from a big Catholic family in the Chicago area. Her parents were married in 1952 and like all good Catholic newlyweds, they worked hard to start a family right away. Unfortunately, Kim's mother was not able to conceive, or so she was told. They adopted two children through Catholic charities, Christine and Bob. They also fostered a son, Bill, from the time he was an infant. While they were never able to legally adopt him, Bill is as much a part of the family as the rest. When she was 30 years old, Kim's mother gave birth to a daughter, Joan, and when she was 38, Kim was born. Adoption and foster care were important to Kim from the time we met and through her family, my eyes were opened to the possibilities for our own family.

Growing up, I knew a couple of people who were adopted, like my best friend in high school, Jennifer, but I had little knowledge of the foster care system. In Jennifer's case, she looks like her adoptive mother. I remember sharing the news of Madison's adoption with Jennifer and she asked me whether we would tell Madison she was adopted. It was all I could do not to laugh out loud. I assured her Madison had no choice but to know she was adopted since we are white and Madison is black. I am sure there were other adoptees from my childhood, but I only knew about a few. Adoption wasn't often talked about when I was growing up and when it was discussed, it was a joyful occasion. Adoption seemed to me as a young person like the ultimate gift with few drawbacks. It never occurred to me that in order for someone to win, someone had to lose in the adoption triad. Several years later my eyes would be opened to the abuse and neglect of millions of children in our very own country as I prepared to become a foster parent.

Given the importance of adoption to Kim's family, we decided to choose the same route as her parents to start our own family. Maybe a foster child would need a forever home. Madison came home to us in 2002 when she was 13 days old. She was the tiniest baby I had ever seen and I was terrified of hurting her. She weighed only three and a half pounds when she arrived. I didn't think babies came this small! In fact, she had weighed more when she was born but lost a lot of weight upon leaving the hospital with her birth mother due to her lactose intolerance, which took a few weeks to diagnose. You should have seen us scampering around the first night for a way to feed this tiny baby since a regular bottle was too big for her mouth. We called area hospitals and organizations for mothers and children, looking for bottles designed for premature babies. They all must have thought we had given birth at home and instead of helping us, they encouraged us to "just bring the baby into the hospital." We finally reached the NICU at St. David's Hospital in Austin and the nurses were willing to help us feed Maddie by giving us a supply of premie bottles.

At home, I waited by the window for Kim to return with the bottles, praying Madison wouldn't wake up because I had no way to feed her save for an eyedropper. It seemed like an eternity before Kim returned with the care package from St. David's. Finally, we were able to feed our daughter. I sat in a green La-Z-Boy recliner in our living room and rocked my sweet angel for hours. She was so tiny! She didn't even have eyelashes and she was so thin. Rocking her in my arms the first night, I wanted to always remember how small and helpless she seemed. I was hooked. I had fallen head over heels in love.

There was never a moment's question as to whether or not we would adopt Madison. She created in me a drive to do most anything to make her world a better place. She taught my parents how to be grandparents. She set the bar for the grandchildren in our family and we continue to marvel everyday at the ways in which she is growing and thriving. A natural leader, Madison is funny, beautiful, athletic, and vivacious. She is the one who gave this book a name. When Maddie was three or four, noticing the difference in our skin color, she pointed out that her own skin was more brown than black. She went on to explain that I wasn't really white but rather pink. My, what a wise little girl I have.

For several years I wondered if I could love another child as much as I loved Madison. It seemed impossible given how crazy I was for her. I lived and breathed Madison! Our family of three was a complete unit. We traveled together, played together, and went to every possible event together. We loved being a family. The older Maddie grew, the more I wanted her to have someone in our family to share this transracial adoption experience. I didn't want hers to be the only brown face on the Christmas card.

Just before Easter in 2007, we received a call from our social worker about providing respite care for another of her foster families. Apparently this family had experienced a death and needed someone to care for their foster child over the Easter weekend. We said yes and met the foster mother on Saturday morning of Easter weekend in the parking lot of Maddie's dance school. It was bitterly cold that Easter and Kim told me to stay in the car with Maddie to stay warm and dry. I watched the foster mother open the minivan door and caught my first glimpse of McKenzie. She stole my heart in the next 30 seconds. Sitting in the car seat, she looked small and frightened, like a baby rabbit.

McKenzie did not smile when her foster mother lifted her from the car. We soon discovered she spoke not a word, despite being 15 months old. I watched her in the rearview mirror as we drove home that Saturday morning and I marveled at her beauty. Her skin was like velvet and she had a high forehead that to me seemed regal. She soon fell asleep in the car, which I have found to be standard operating procedure for children in foster care; they arrive in our care emotionally exhausted.

We spent the weekend playing and laughing with Madison, marveling at the way McKenzie was relaxing as each hour passed. We celebrated Easter with close friends. I was in heaven, mothering these two little girls. I swore to Kim at the end of the weekend that I was going to find a way to make McKenzie part of our forever family. It took four whole days to have her case transferred to our home. A few months later, we consummated McKenzie's adoption.

I thought our family was complete after adding McKenzie to our brood. Imagine our great surprise when the call came in May 2008 that McKenzie's birth mother had delivered another baby girl. Were we interested? Are you kidding? In ten minutes we made the decision to bring a new baby home, this time direct from the hospital. It seemed like an eternity before the social worker arrived at our front door with our new bundle of joy. McKenzie fell asleep sitting upright on the couch waiting for her baby sister, whom we would call Morgan, to arrive.

Kim and I make a great team when it comes to caring for a child in need. In one hour, we had newborn clothes washed and dried, the crib assembled, the car seat ready, and the entire house vacuumed. Okay, the vacuuming part was more to settle my nerves, but the house looked great by the time she arrived. Several neighbors anxiously waited with us and the poor social worker was mobbed when he pulled into the driveway. I remember thinking, "Just give me my baby!"

The neighbors danced around Morgan, sharing in our celebration. Madison and McKenzie were so excited to see the baby, each wanting to hold her and kiss her head. Morgan slept through it all. Eventually, the neighbors left and the girls went to bed. Kim and I sat on our bed for hours watching Morgan breathe, wondering what to name her and marveling at the magnitude of the day's surprise. I never thought I would be a mother. I knew as a teenager I would not marry a man and have babies the traditional way. I just assumed I would never have children. When Madison came to us, I thought it was the greatest miracle of my life. When McKenzie found her way into my heart, I thought life could not get any better. She was the rich, maple syrup on an already delicious stack of pancakes. And now we had Morgan! Life is good.

So now I am the proud mother of three of the most amazing little girls ever born. I didn't receive any training on how to meet the physical and social needs of these precious brown babies. I have learned everything I know through the kindness of both strangers and friends. I own dozens of books on adoption and transracial parenting. I have read them cover to cover looking for practical answers and found very few. The authors are very knowledgeable, scholarly people, but only one had raised a child of color in a

Caucasian home. After reading each of these books, I still didn't know how to comb hair or how to incorporate another culture into my home or how to answer the hard questions. I needed another mom, a girlfriend, to show me the way! And so here I am, sharing what I have learned the hard way with you, in hopes that I will save you time and heartache as you go about the business of raising your own miracle.

More and more parents are accepting the challenge of raising a child who not only was born from another womb but who does not even share their ethnicity. According to a *New York Times* article, "Overcoming Adoption's Racial Barriers," by Lynette Clemetson and Ron Nixon (August 17, 2006), "Laws that make it illegal for federally financed agencies to deny adoptions based on race have removed barriers for white families to adopt black children." The authors found that the rate of adoptions of black children in foster care by white families had increased dramatically. "The total number of white households in the 2000 census that reported adopting a black child is still small, but experts say the numbers are increasing." The graph contained in the same article showed only 14% of adoptions by white households in 1998 were of black children from foster care. The percentage nearly doubled by 2004 when 26% of adoptions from foster care by white households were of black children.

The numbers have been difficult to track until recently since transracial adoptions were never officially counted until the 2000 census. I was thrilled to complete the section of the most recent census form that asked about the ethnicity of our adopted children. Getting an accurate figure for the number of transracially adopted children in our country may prompt an increase in funding for post-adoption services and better prepare prospective parents.

It is my sincere desire to pass on the lessons I have learned to other pink parents to address the cultural, physical, spiritual, and emotional needs of their African-American children. If I can help even one parent by showing them how to comb a daughter's hair or how to find their place in a community to which they do not belong, I will be thrilled. Well-intentioned adoptive parents eventually learn that to love a child is not enough. Human beings are complex creatures and our children have needs that we are not prepared to address because these needs were not part of our life experience.

I am not an expert in the fields of child development or child psychology. There are no initials after my name. I am a mother in the trenches, walking the walk every day as I raise the brown babies lovingly placed in my pink arms so many years ago. It was never my plan to create a transracial family, but I give thanks every day for the chance to take the road less traveled. It is an honor to share the story of my family and the lessons we have learned along the way. I will tell this story as long as parents are willing to listen, until there is no need to explain race relations or white privilege, and every child has a home. My mission is to make this world a better place for my own children and others like them.

# Chapter 1

## What Is Transracial Adoption?

*When you put faith, hope, and love together, you can raise positive kids in a negative world. — Zig Ziglar*

Transracial adoption is a heavy term, loaded with emotion and opinion. Simply put, transracial adoption refers to children of one race being adopted by parents of another race. In most cases of transracial adoption in the U.S., Caucasians are adopting children from impoverished countries, from the U.S. welfare system, or through private agencies that place U.S. children. While both African-American and Caucasian families adopt at a similar pace, there are more African-American children in the foster care system, thus increasing the odds of Caucasian families parenting children of a different race. Given the volatile nature of race relations in our country, it is not surprising how emotionally charged the issue of transracial adoption can be. Before exploring what works and does not work in transracial families, let us take a moment to understand how transracial adoption came to be the way it is today.

The relationship between blacks and whites in this country has been problematic from the start. Africans were brought to the United States against their will, enslaved and oppressed. The abuse continued for generations. The idea of raising each other's children may seem intimately frightening to some. Racism still exists today, decades after the Civil Rights Movement of the 1960s, and for many white Americans, this comes as a surprise. After all, we recently elected a black President for the first time in the history of our country, so how racist could we be?

Well, let me just tell you, pretty darn racist!

Yes, our country has come a long way, but we aren't there yet. If you have never experienced racism, adopting a black child is a great way to find out what it feels like to be judged or disliked before you ever have the chance to speak. My daughter Madison is in the first grade and attended the after-school program of the YMCA. I received a call one afternoon from the onsite director who told me there had been an incident in which two little boys told Madison she could not be beautiful because she was black. I was horrified that children as young as kindergarten and first grade could believe such nonsense. Fortunately, Madison didn't believe them and told the boys exactly how beautiful she is.

One of the many benefits of white privilege is not having to think about our race because we are the majority. For many, racism exists only in the media and has never personally touched their lives. This will change with the addition of a black member to your family. I was well into my first transracial adoption before I learned the magnitude of white privilege, which is addressed later in this book.

Reporter Jeff Gammage of the *Philadelphia Inquirer* addressed the racism issue in his May 2006 article, "For Adoptees, Racial Divide Still Wide." As the arrival of children adopted from countries like China, Guatemala, India and Liberia creates thousands of new multiracial families each year, Gammage notes that "adoption today is a rainbow of color and country." Yet, he says, it is the pairing of African-American children and white parents that sparks the most intense debate, because it touches on the still-tender wound of slavery, one Gammage describes as our country's "primal wound."

"Though white people might view interracial adoption as evidence of societal progress," says Gammage, "for many black people it is painful harkening back to a time when their ancestors were treated as property.... Love may be color-blind, but society is not."

It was never my plan to create a transracial family. It just happened that way. And it was surprisingly easy. In the initial home study we were asked if we had a racial preference, but that is the only time the subject ever came up. Foster children came and went from our home, mostly black and a few Hispanic. I cannot recall a social worker ever asking if we had questions about parenting a child of a different race or offering help or resources concerning culture or race. When the parental rights of the birth parents were terminated, no one ever brought up the subject of race or questioned our desire to be a forever family. The system truly seemed to be color-blind.

Was it always this way? The answer: Absolutely not!

Adoption has come a long way over the decades, especially in the area of transracial adoption. In the early 1900s, families tended to take care of unplanned pregnancies on their own, rarely involving the outside world. Without the benefit of birth control, women often had more children than they could handle and in many cases, family members would step in to parent those children. Orphanages existed but there was nothing like the foster care system today.

Transracial adoptions were rare before the 1960s due to the legal separation of the races. When social workers did become involved in the adoption process during the mid-1900s, the goal was to match as many characteristics of the child with the adoptive parents. This seems like a reasonable practice to me until you take into account how many children of color were in need of a home and then things got tricky.

The Civil Rights Movement opened the door to a new understanding of race relations and the value of integration and in doing so, opened the door to new homes for many children. Researchers Simon and Alstein, in their 1977 book on *Transracial Adoption*,[1] state there were 2574 black children adopted by white families in 1968, which sounds like a good start until you read what happened in 1972 when the National Association of Black Social Workers (NABSW) took a stand on the issue. In their *Position Statement on Transracial Adoption*, the group stated, "The National Association of Black Social Workers has taken a vehement stand against the placement of black children in white homes for any reason. We affirm the inviolable position of black children in black families where they belong physically, psychologically, and culturally in order that they receive the total sense of themselves and develop a sound projection of their future."[2][3]

This was, by far, the biggest blow to transracial adoption in the history of our country. The opinion of the National Association of Black Social Workers was adopted by the majority of folks involved in the facilitation of adoptions and while transracial placements still took place during the 1970s and '80s, the numbers were low. Finally, someone challenged the opinion of the association and the subject was revisited in the early 1990s. Harvard legal professors Elizabeth Bartholet and Randall Kennedy began talking about transracial adoption and researching whether or not the civil rights of black children were being violated through race matching in adoption. In his 1994 paper, "Orphans of Separatism: The Painful Politics of Transracial Adoption," Randall Kennedy states, "What parentless children need are not 'white,' 'black,' 'yellow,' 'brown,' or 'red' parents but *loving* parents." [4]

Randall Kennedy paved the way for Congress to pass the Multiethnic Placement Act (MEPA) in 1994, followed by the Interethnic Adoption Provisions, which banned the use of race in adoption or foster care placement as the sole criterion for matching families and threatened the loss of federal funding and other stiff penalties if this ban was violated. These are the acts that make it possible for my family to exist. I am tremendously thankful these laws were passed and that my family has the opportunity to exist. At the same time, I recognize that the National Association of Black Social Workers was trying to protect the interests of black children. I appreciate their dedication to these children, but I want to prove them wrong. I want to do the best job I possibly can in raising children who will someday be part of the larger world. As my grandmother used to say, "Don't throw out the baby with the bathwater!" In my opinion, this is exactly what happened when NABSW decided only black parents could raise black children.

The system has come a long way. It is not perfect, but we're making strides all the time to make the world of adoption a better place. As we look ahead, it is important to remember how we reached this point. All three of my transracial adoptions were relatively easy, save for the usual dips and curves of working with the foster care system. I owe a debt of gratitude to those families, researchers, and lawmakers who paved the way for me.

> *The conclusion is clear — black children are still over-represented in the foster care system. In addition, the inability to address race as part of the process has left transracial families unprepared to tackle the very real challenges of helping their children form a racial identity and learn skills to deal with racism on an individual and institutional level. Who does this hurt? The same kids MEPA was intended to help.*
>
> *The bottom line is that transracial adoption is the intersection of some fundamental things: race, class, identity, and family. It forces us to look critically at who we are, what we believe about families, how we perceive the world we live in, and what comprises justice and injustice.*
>
> *Listening to my daughter chatter away as she applied lip gloss to my lips (and cheeks and nose) I never imagined that I would be seriously contemplating issues such as these. If you choose to parent transracially, your family will be intimately tied to larger concerns that have few clear answers. You will no longer have the luxury of looking the other way, of benign indifference, of hoping something will change someday. When you choose this child, you choose everything about them, and beliefs and actions related to race, class, identity and family become not an issue for them but an issue for us.*
>
> *— Aimee Estep, Austin, TX; mother of two*

# Chapter 2

## Is Transracial Adoption Right For Me?

*The strength of motherhood is greater than natural laws.*
— Barbara Kingsolver

I grew up in South Mississippi in the 1980s when race was everything. My family moved from Plano, Texas, to Hattiesburg, Miss., in '85 and I enrolled in the seventh grade at our neighborhood school. The first day of school, I was shocked to discover two things: there was no air conditioning in the entire school, and there were more black faces in my classes than I had ever seen in my life. At the time, the school district was involved in a school integration lawsuit that would last many years, and the terms of integration were still being worked out. Maintaining a racial balance of 60:40 in neighborhood schools (that is 60% black to 40% white) wasn't easy. This was the topic of the nightly local news most days of the week for what seemed like forever. By the ninth grade, my friends and I would be bused to a school across town in a neighborhood that looked like a different country.

Racism lived on both sides of the track. It sat at the lunch table with you at school. It was there at the dinner table in your home. It was present at every PTA meeting. Race was a big deal but you didn't talk about it in public and certainly never in mixed company. Maybe this was the reason why, starting in junior high, I read everything I could find about the Civil Rights Movement. I wanted to understand why things were the way they were. I wasn't born in Mississippi; I had moved there and found myself an observer of the strangest social scenario I had ever seen. There were black students in every one of my classes, yet black people did not attend my church or live in my neighborhood or go to the same birthday parties with me, and I wanted to know why. Oftentimes, the tension between the races was palpable. I was horrified to learn about Mississippi's role in the Civil Rights Movement yet fascinated and perplexed at the way discrimination and segregation were still taking place twenty years later. You were either black or white and the two rarely mixed outside of the classroom.

In high school, April and I were on the newspaper staff together and in many of the same classes. April was funny, smart, popular, beautiful, and black. Her family was different from other black families. Her father was on the school board and would eventually become the mayor of our town. April's uncle was a popular local minister. Her family was well educated and well connected and lived in a beautiful home in downtown Hattiesburg. It was through my relationship with April that I saw firsthand the pressure black students bore from their own community not to be "too white." Black high-school students were starting to wear shirts that read, "It's a Black Thing," and racial pride was growing. Looking back, April was one of the bravest people I knew in high school because she walked a fine line between black and white. Today, April's father is running for governor of the state of Mississippi. In the twenty-first century, a man of color has never held this highest state office. Imagine! Looking back, I realize April and I were more alike than we were different, but it didn't feel like it at the time.

One day, as I was waiting for my appointment at the tanning salon after school, an affluent white woman walked in with a black baby boy on her hip. I nearly passed out. What was she doing? What was she thinking? Was she adopting him? It was as if I'd seen a bird and a fish embracing. I was in complete shock that there in Mississippi two people of different races could love each other as intimately as this mother and child obviously did. Perhaps a bird and a fish can fall in love, I thought, but where will they live? I don't know what happened with this baby, but I do know he didn't live with this family for long.

I wonder if people look at my family the same way. Of course, I live in a different time and place now, a place where minds are more open and the subject of race is not as contentious as it was in my youth. And, in case you are wondering, I would eventually discover an answer to the question about where the bird and the fish can live. The bird and the fish live in a place they create together in the midst of both air and water. Not many animals (or people) can live here, but love makes it possible.

In 2001 when I first applied to foster a child, the memories of racial tension from my youth were still strong and I told the social worker performing our home study that I didn't think I could raise an

African-American child. My parents still lived in Mississippi at the time. How would we ever visit them in what was still a very racist corner of the country? While I had moved to a more liberal city, I didn't think I had it in me to parent a child of color.

But what did I know? Either the social worker totally misunderstood me or the all-knowing Higher Power interceded on my behalf, because black children started rolling into my home a few months later. In the eight years I have been a foster parent, I have parented only one Caucasian child and one Hispanic child. The rest have been African-American. Like so many other adoptive parents, I received little training on parenting a child of a different race.

Susan Griffin, an adoptive mother of twelve and a social worker for Family By Choice, says she received no training at all to care for her children of color. The same is true for other parents like Jennifer Graf, Carole Boeck, and Jennifer Danvers who adopted through the foster care system in Texas. All three mothers say the diversity training they received prior to becoming a parent was minimal. Tricia Kakalec of Brooklyn, N.Y., was fortunate to receive three hours of training through the private agency she used to adopt her son Julian. All of these mothers told me the primary way they learned to care for their brown babies was by networking with other parents. Most Caucasian parents of African-American children surveyed for this book agree they need more people of color in their inner circle.

I didn't think I was equipped to be the parent of a child of a different race until I became one. In hindsight, growing up in Mississippi prepared me to mother my children because it gave me firsthand experience of African-American culture. I had witnessed the separate and distinct cultures of the races. I had observed a rich tradition of heritage and pride within the black community of my hometown, with just as many rituals, rules of etiquette, and social stigmas as the white community. There was no way I could raise an African-American child the same way I would parent a white one because I knew there was a cultural inheritance that I needed to acknowledge.

My identity as a lesbian has helped me embrace my role in a multicultural family. My sexuality makes me a member of a minority group. I am used to being under the microscope. I am used to people staring at my partner and me when we go out as a couple. I have come to expect that some people may not like me when they find out who

I am and who I love. There are very few laws in place to protect my family legally and financially because my family is not acknowledged by the government as a real one, despite our being in a committed relationship for ten years, owning a home and two cars together, paying taxes, joining the PTA, actively participating in our Homeowner's Association, and adopting three children. The laws that do exist pertaining to gay and lesbian people came about as the result of long, exhausting, and expensive battles in the courtrooms and the conference rooms. Gay and lesbian people struggle in much the same way as African-Americans did during the Civil Rights Movement (and still do). There is much common ground here.

In my mind, the Civil Rights Movement took place in my own family when I was in the third grade. That year, my family went home to Richmond, Va., for Thanksgiving. It was a tension-filled day, waiting for what I thought was going to be a typical holiday dinner, but a bigger drama was unfolding among the adults of my family. My mother's oldest sister, Gail, was coming home for the first time in many years. I had never met Gail and I could hardly wait to meet her. I waited by the window, my stomach turning with excitement every time a car traveled down Bowles Lane.

Gail and my grandparents had become estranged for a number of reasons but the biggest was her love of a black man. I don't know the details of the healing or the negotiations that took place to make it possible for Gail to come to Thanksgiving that year. I was just a kid and I was thrilled to finally meet her. I remember watching her small blue hatchback pull up in front of the house. She emerged from the car with platinum blond hair, so totally different from her sisters'. My mother told me disapprovingly, it was "straight from a bottle." I had no idea what that meant, but I thought Gail looked like a movie star. I don't remember what was said when she walked through the front door or if anyone cried. What I do remember is taking dozens of pictures in front of the fireplace with my mother and her sisters. Our family was complete because Gail had come home.

Gail later married George, who was black, and in doing so paved the way for my family to incorporate people of color into the inner sanctum of our tribe. My grandparents have both passed away now. They lived in a nursing home for the last few years of their lives. Gail and George lived the closest to the nursing home and the responsibility of my grandparents' care fell to them. Gail and George visited often, always bringing special treats and taking care of every need. George was a good man, to have done all he did for my grandparents, and it was obvious how much they loved him at the end. Having an open and accepting family is vitally important in making the decision to parent children of a different race.

The other big factor that helped us in becoming a transracial family is our openness to change. In 2003, Kim and I were trying to adopt Maddie. During Thanksgiving dinner at my parents' house that year, a discussion took place around the dining table about transracial parenting. The question was asked, "Do you know how to raise a child to be a strong black woman in this country?" The simple answer is no. I have never been a black woman and I never will be. I do not have all the life skills and experiences to impart to my daughter that she will need in order to navigate the race-conscious world in which we live. I would have to rely on an army of powerful black women to serve as role models. If I was going to adopt this child of color, I would have to be open to changing my life to incorporate people, ideas, traditions, and practices that may not feel comfortable to me because they are not part of my life experience. The willingness to change and the ability to open not just my heart but also my mind to other ways of living and thinking have proven to be monumentally important in the success of our family.

Making the decision to adopt is a giant one. Whatever the reason you choose to adopt, a bigger decision must be made regarding who you will adopt. "I always wanted a brown family because I knew children of color were harder to place," says Jennifer Danvers, adoptive mother of three children. For Tricia Kakalec the probability of parenting across the color line was high. "I told the social worker during my home study that I was open to any race. My friends later predicted I would be placed with an African-American child because I told the woman I was open. Sure enough, I was immediately placed with an African-American boy." Jennifer Graf, mother of an eight-year-old African-American daughter, had a similar experience. "I did not have anyone in mind in particular when I decided to adopt, but I knew placing a child of color was more difficult. I had no worries about being able to expose my child to a different culture. I have a very diverse family and am an active member of an historically black church," explains Graf.

Transracial parenting is not for everyone. Like marriage or buying a home, it should not be entered into lightly. It is absolutely necessary to take a personal inventory to determine your capabilities and limitations. Once you have assessed yourself individually and together as a couple (should that be the case), take a look at your family. Parenting any child is never easy. Parenting an adopted child comes with its own set of issues. Parenting across the color line adds a whole new dimension to the mix. Are you ready?

Grab your Number 2 pencil and get started on these two light-hearted quizzes that will get you thinking about the issues involved. Answers are given at the end of the chapter.

## Quiz 1: Assessing Your Knowledge of African-American Culture

Quiz 1 will get you thinking about a few issues that are important to blacks and how connected you are to the black community where you live.

1.  Other than the *Cosby Show*, name five television portrayals of upper middle-class families or individuals of color.

2.  What does a perm do to African-American hair?
    a.  Makes the hair super-curly.
    b.  Loosens the curl so the hair straightens.
    c.  Makes the hair wavy.

3.  Name five individuals from black history and their accomplishments, other than Martin Luther King, Jr. and Barack Obama.

4.  Black women earn what percentage of what white males earn?
    a.  62%
    b.  102% because of affirmative action
    c.  88%

5.  What is institutional racism?
    a.  A race where institutions compete against each other, like Dell vs. Apple in a three legged race.
    b.  Racism that went crazy and is now in prison.
    c.  Racism that has become part of the many institutions in our society such as banking, education, media, and business.

6.  In your own community, name as many of these African-American resources as you can:
    a.  Churches.
    b.  Hair salons or barbershops.
    c.  Politicians.
    d.  Neighborhoods.

7.  How many people of color do you see on a daily basis?

8.  How many of these people do you interact with in a meaningful way?

9.  Name five things you like about being your race.

10. How often do you hear racist jokes from friends, colleagues, or family members?

## Quiz 2: Personal Inventory

Quiz 2 will get you thinking about your own personal qualities.

| | | | |
|---|---|---|---|
| 1. | I consider myself to be a minority or I have a strong sense of what it is like to be a member of a minority group. | **Yes** | **No** |
| 2. | I am comfortable being the focus of unsolicited attention. | **Yes** | **No** |
| 3. | I am comfortable talking to strangers about personal issues. | **Yes** | **No** |
| 4. | I am open to change, accepting of new ideas. | **Yes** | **No** |
| 5. | My family is diverse with more than one culture or has displayed a willingness to accept other cultures. | **Yes** | **No** |
| 6. | I am comfortable asking for help. | **Yes** | **No** |
| 7. | I have a do-what-it-takes-to-get-the-job-done attitude. | **Yes** | **No** |
| 8. | I have a strong support system to help me on this life-changing journey. | **Yes** | **No** |
| 9. | I feel secure enough in myself to be in uncomfortable situations. | **Yes** | **No** |
| 10. | Hard work does not scare me. | **Yes** | **No** |

**Quiz 1 Answers:** 2. B; 4. A; 5. C.

**Quiz 2 Answers:** If you answered Yes to eight or more of these questions, congratulations. You are a flexible thinker, open to change and new experiences, adaptable and willing to do what needs to be done in any situation. Transracial adoption may be for you.

If you answered No to five or more questions, then you may want to think twice about transracial adoption.

# Chapter 3

## Best Practices of Transracial Families

*Nothing you ever do is wasted on a child.* — Garrison Keillor

Most of my professional life has been spent in sales. Specifically, I have been a travel agent since I was 21. I am a natural salesperson. I love to sell! I find it thrilling to identify a need and locate the correct product/location/idea/answer to meet the need. My career in sales started early in life, as my mother tells it. I once set up a sidewalk rock stand (think lemonade stand) to sell my collection of rocks. I was maybe four years old and my parents thought it truly pitiful to watch me sitting on the sidewalk with my rocks, that is, until I came into the house with a wad of cash and an empty box! I once had a manager tell me I could get someone excited about going to hell!

One thing I like about salespeople is their habit of sharing best practices. I enjoy getting together with other salespeople to talk about what works best and sharing with one another how we have been successful. I have found this practice to be even more helpful in my parenting. It is tremendously beneficial to hear from other parents how they have improved the smooth running of their family or incorporated new ideas or methods to address the parenting challenges we all face.

After many years of listening to parents who have adopted transracially and even more years as the mother of African-American children, here is my list of best practices for parenting across the color line (in no particular order).

## Create a Village

There is an African proverb that says, "It takes a village to raise a child." Never was this more true than for transracial families. I would like to think I know it all, but I don't. I turn to the "Village" for help at most turns in the road. In our family, the Village includes godparents, members of our community of faith, our adoption therapist, pediatrician, teachers, child-care providers, support groups, babysitters, hairstylists and friends. The Village is your support system and should be racially diverse.

> *I was raised to believe you don't go outside of the family*
> *for help. You rely on your people in times of trouble.*
> *Obviously, this doesn't work too well in my [transracial]*
> *family. We need other people! I am getting better about*
> *asking for help. The adoption agency I used is very helpful*
> *and I am learning to call other foster/adoptive parents in*
> *the area when I need a hand. Believe me, it doesn't come*
> *naturally [to me]. I have to work on asking for help.*
> *— Jennifer Danvers, Taylor, TX; mother of three*

When my youngest daughter, Morgan, was eight months old, she was diagnosed in the doctor's office with RSV. RSV is a dangerous respiratory condition that can be fatal for infants. This happened late in the day on a Friday afternoon. We were panicked, to say the very least, when our wonderful pediatrician sent us immediately to Dell Children's Hospital with a fistful of orders. While driving down the freeway towards the hospital, it occurs to me that we have two other children who must be picked up from school and cared for. I immediately call a member of the Village to explain the situation. Without blinking an eye, she goes to my house, packs a bag for each child, picks them up from school, and entertains them for the weekend while we focus our attention on Morgan.

I cannot imagine what we would have done in this situation if we didn't have systems in place for an emergency. Whether your children are black or white, adopted or biological, stuff happens and you need help as a parent. Reduce the amount of stress in your life by having people to call in any emergency. And not just any people but people who love your kids.

> *When we were adopting our kids back in the 1970s,*
> *there wasn't much support for transracial families.*
> *COAC (Council on Adoptable Children) was our Village.*
> *— Susan Griffith, Jonestown, TX; mother of 12*

## Find a Support Group

Becoming a mother is a life-changing event. Unfortunately, I didn't carry my girls through nine months of pregnancy and have limited, if any, history about the birth family. I do, however, have an endless supply of questions. Is this normal? Why does she do this? Is this a race thing? Is this an adoption thing? Or is it a four-year-old thing?

When I became a mother, I began to reflect on my own childhood. I saw my childhood with a mother's eyes and realized the gift I have in my own mother. When I became the mother of an African-American daughter, I saw every person of color through a mother's eyes. I found an opportunity to address my own fears and prejudices. To do that, I needed a safe place to process my thoughts and feelings about race. I needed a loving place to ask questions I suspected were totally ridiculous but needed answering all the same. I wanted to swap stories with other parents facing the same challenges as me. I needed to learn how to comb hair, prevent ashy skin, and incorporate my daughter's culture into my home. I needed to find friends for my kids whose families looked like ours.

Madison was just about a year old when we heard through the Child Protective Services (CPS) grapevine that a support group for adoptive and foster parents was forming at a local church. More specifically, this group wanted to gather together transracial families to help them cope with the challenges of parenting across the color line. I signed up immediately. Though I wasn't familiar with this church and didn't know anyone there, I counted down the days to the first meeting.

The group was led by two church members, Ora Houston and Dr. Ruth McRoy. Ora is a beautiful lady with short, gray hair who I could tell had been fierce in the Civil Rights Movement. She is a community activist and dedicated Episcopalian. Ruth is a professor at the University of Texas in the School of Social Work. We later discovered she is a leading authority in this country on the subject of adoption. Imagine my surprise sitting next to such a giant in the adoption community! Ora and Ruth recognized an increased number of transracial families attending services at St. James Episcopal Church and wanted to create a group to support these parents. I will forever be thankful to these ladies for doing so.

The room was packed for the first meeting. I was amazed to see so many of us! Straight families and gay families with children in every shade of the rainbow were present. We went around the room to introduce ourselves. The conversation was light and friendly until someone started crying. This woman was exhausted, distressed, and struggling to meet the needs of her children with very few tools at her disposal. The minute she started crying, I knew the group was going to be a good one because a sense of honesty and trust immediately filled the room. We understood each other in ways our friends and family members couldn't because they had not walked in our shoes.

Years later, I still attend the monthly meetings of Parenting Across Color. I am tremendously thankful for these friends who help me through every stage of parenting. My friends from PAC have celebrated with me the arrival of each new child into our home, cried with me when difficult decisions had to be made, and come to my rescue in times of crisis. Through the speakers, I have learned to comb hair, advocate for my kids in the school system, understand precocious puberty in minority children, and so much more. Everyone should be so lucky to find such a group. Go look for one now. If you can't find one, consider starting one of your own. There is information in the back of this book about starting your own chapter of Parenting Across Color.

> *Raising kids is a whole lot of work and being a transracial*
> *family was more work than we could have imagined.*
> *Networking with other families was the best way for us to*
> *determine if we were experiencing racial issues,*
> *adoption issues, or five-year-old issues. I don't think*
> *we would have made it without Parenting Across Color.*
> *— Carole Boeck, Austin, TX; mother of twins*

## Seek Opportunities to Be the Minority

It was a typical Saturday afternoon in March. I walked with my daughter into a youth complex in East Austin where a friend's birthday party is being held. It took a few minutes to find the right party room, so McKenzie and I walked around the enormous facility until we found her friend. I was holding onto McKenzie with one hand and the gift with the other. I could feel the stares. I could hear the whispers. Both became more obvious when we walked into the party room. The hair on the back of my neck was standing tall. I was painfully aware of the size of the room, the number of people in it, and my own discomfort. McKenzie's friend ran to hug her and gave me a quick squeeze. I smiled at the parents and said friendly hellos. As I turned to find either a seat or a friend, I saw the firing squad of grandparents, aunties, neighbors, cousins, and friends who were dying to know exactly who I was with this black child. They sat shoulder to shoulder in a long row of chairs, staring at me. I was the only white face in the building.

No one offered me a seat. No one even smiled. A lesser woman would have fled the building, but not me. I am a mother who will do anything for my children, including put myself in an uncomfortable situation that painfully reminds me how my children sometimes feel in our family and in the world. I am a Caucasian mother raising three African-American daughters who were adopted through the foster care system. Looks and whispers are commonplace for our transracial family but it is rare that I face an unfriendly room. I usually don't give people a choice as to whether or not they will like me. I try hard to make a friend or find a connection wherever I go and this day was no exception. By the end of the party, at least two people were smiling at me and five more even spoke to me. That's okay because the goal for the day was to allow McKenzie to attend her friend's birthday party and we did. McKenzie had a blast. I would rather be the one who is uncomfortable than allow my child to feel out of place.

I am always looking for opportunities for my daughters to be in the majority. I am always counting brown faces and pink faces to find the right mix where my girls can be comfortable in their surroundings. All of my children attend or attended Mt. Sinai Christian Academy, a preschool in a black church. For several years, Madison took dance classes at a school on the other side of town where there were only two pink faces in the room. We were recently invited to join an African dance troupe with traditional drummers that meets every Saturday. We attend a church with more brown faces than pink.

It isn't easy. It isn't always comfortable for me. But that's okay because I don't mind being uncomfortable. What I mind is having my children feel uncomfortable. Transracial parenting means sticking your neck out, taking some risks, and doing what is in the best interest of your kiddos. Don't be afraid! More often than not, people will surprise you. I can't tell you how many times I have embarrassed myself or looked a fool for the sake of getting what I need to meet my children's needs. How could anyone fault you for loving a child too much?

## Consider a Sibling Group

Recently our family took a cruise through the Inside Passage of Alaska where we encountered another transracial family. They were from Vermont, where the African-American population is low. This family had adopted three children of color in a predominantly Caucasian state. The mother told me with great conviction that she believed Caucasian parents adopting African-American children should adopt a sibling group or consider adopting other children of color so they won't be lonely in their own family. I completely agreed.

Madison was an only child for four years when we decided to adopt again. It was a big decision to even consider the possibility of adding another child to our family. We now have three daughters and we, the parents, are in the racial minority. My girls think this is very funny and I am happy they have each other to share this wild ride of being in a transracial family. As empathetic and sensitive as I am, I can never know what it feels like to be the only anything in a family. Fortunately, my daughters have two sisters who know exactly what it feels like.

## Introduce Your Child to His or Her Culture

Cultural or racial identity is learned and doesn't come naturally to any child. Since I don't have the life experiences to teach my daughters their racial identity, I must find other ways for them to learn. For me, this lesson is just as important as making sure my kids brush their teeth every day and learn right from wrong.

When Madison was 14 months old, a co-worker of Kim's told us about a child development center called Mt. Sinai Christian Academy. This preschool is associated with Mt. Sinai Missionary Baptist Church where Kim's co-worker attended services and had enrolled her own children in the school. The church was 99% African-American. (Though I have never seen a white member, I am leaving 1% for the benefit of the doubt.) We knew Madison would start to recognize the differences between our skin colors around age three. We decided the best way to prepare for that revelation was to surround her by people who looked just like she did. It was one of the most intimidating experiences of my life, walking into the school the first day for a tour and to enroll our daughter, but I knew it was the right decision. Putting our personal level of comfort aside, we enrolled Madison at Mt. Sinai.

It took a couple of weeks for the teachers and parents to reach their own level of comfort with our family. Not only were we white, but we were also two women raising an African-American daughter.

I am the first to admit we took some getting used to. I laugh when I think about those first few months. I was nervous and uncomfortable and I thought the teachers were too harsh. Part of that struggle was finding my place in my daughter's world. The other part was being a first-time mother.

I consider Mt. Sinai to be our home now. Madison enrolled in 2004 and finished the preschool program in 2008 when she moved to kindergarten in our neighborhood public school. When McKenzie came home to us in 2007, we introduced her to our extended Mt. Sinai family and they welcomed her into the flock. She is finishing her last year in the preschool program and will enroll at "big-girl school" with Maddie in the fall. Morgan, our surprise baby, is in the Baby Moses class where Madison and McKenzie both began their schooling at Mt. Sinai. For six years, I have driven 30 minutes in each direction twice a day in order for my daughters to attend Mt. Sinai. If that isn't commitment, I don't know what is.

It feels impossible to adequately express how much I appreciate this preschool. The director Kay Fowler and her staff have loved, supported, and embraced our family in ways I could never have imagined. We have been given a community where everyone feels safe to be whom God intended. My children were given the Christian education I wanted them to have and the daily cultural lessons I needed them to have. When Madison would say grace before dinner, she would sometimes "freestyle" by speaking from her heart with a raised voice, a raised hand, and a firm grip on the table with the other hand. Madison knows who she is and I can say with confidence she learned that from Mt. Sinai. Through Mt. Sinai, I have learned to walk the walk. I have found a comfortable place in my own skin in the black community. Where is your Mt. Sinai?

## Find a Church Home

Our family lives in a very white suburb of Austin. We live here because the housing is more affordable than in the city of Austin. Being a gay Christian family means we cannot walk into any ole church on the corner and expect to be welcomed, so finding the right one for us took some time. I point this out only to share with you that the process of finding a church home is never easy and being different makes the process a tad more difficult. Before having children, we were dedicated members of the Metropolitan Community Church of Austin (MCCA), which is accepting of all people. The congregation of MCCA is primarily white with a large Hispanic population and a few African-Americans. Much to my delight, we were invited to attend St. James Episcopal Church, where our monthly Parenting Across Color group meets. St. James is truly a melting pot. There are black people, white people, and brown people. There are wealthy people and those of modest means. There are straight people and gay people. St. James is a perfect fit for our family, even though neither one of us has ever been Episcopalian. We found a church home that meets the needs of our children and we, the parents, will adjust accordingly. The congregation of St. James provides my children with the examples I hope they will follow in life. My daughters are able to see every week what it looks like to be proud and faithful women of color.

## Read and Educate Yourself

I am amazed at the number of books available for both parents and children alike on the subject of adoption. It is easy to become overwhelmed by the options! I have found reading to be a great source of information about everything from adoption in general to attachment issues and transracial issues. One of my favorite places to find all things adoption-related is Tapestry Books (www.tapestrybooks.com), which offers something for everyone. It is important to remember there are as many books as there are opinions. I used to scare myself reading some of the many stories of transracial adoptions gone wrong. Now I choose to focus on the positive and leave the negative stories for the what-never-to-do part of my brain.

I consider *Inside Transracial Adoption* by Beth Hall and Gail Steinberg to be the Bible on the subject of families like mine. I have read it a couple of times and think it offers something for everyone adopting a child of color. *Black Baby White Hands: A View from the Crib* by Jaiya John is a great story from the perspective of the child. I recently discovered a true gem of a book in *I'm Chocolate, You're Vanilla: Raising Healthy Black and Bi-Racial Children in a Race Conscious World* by Marguerite Wright. These are just a few of the books that have made a significant impact on my parenting. I am looking forward to the release of *Growing Up Black in White* by my friend Kevin Hofmann, as I believe he has a powerful story of transracial adoption to share with the world, one that is refreshingly positive.

My friend Janie Cravens is a social worker who has taken part in more than 5000 adoptions over the course of her 30-year career. I recently heard Janie say to a group of adoptive parents, "Become a Ph.D. in what it feels like to be adopted." To me, that meant immersing myself in as much information about the adoption experience as possible. I have come across many articles and books that have not been a good match for my particular adoption scenario, but I keep reading. Again, who wants to take a gamble on the well-being of their baby? Definitely maintain a subscription to *Adoptive Families* magazine, which covers issues of transracial adoption in every issue, including the answers to the toughest of questions.

Another friend, Jennifer Graf, is a single adoptive mother of Madelyn, age eight. Jennifer is a teacher and avid reader who maintains an incredible list of resources on the topic of African heritage. The list includes multimedia, books, magazine articles and much, much more. For a sampling from her list, see the Resource section located at the back of this book.

To educate yourself about black culture, subscribe to traditionally black magazines like *Essence* or *Jet*. Join the National Association for the Advancement of Colored People (NAACP) and look for the local NAACP on the internet to see what upcoming activities might interest your child, as well as the whole family. It is vitally important to stay in the know about issues and concerns facing your child's race.

> *We made a point to expose our kids to the history of their culture. We took a Civil Rights tour, visiting Birmingham and Selma, Alabama. We visited museums and went to church bazaars to pick up black Christmas ornaments and tree toppers. And, of course, we networked at NACAC (North American Council on Adoptable Children) and COAC (Council on Adoptable Children).*
> *— Bobbie Kerr, McKinney, TX; mother of four*

## Find a Hair Salon or Barbershop

Check the local phone book, use the internet to find options in your area, or ask for recommendations from members of your support group or black friends. Not only is finding your hair-care headquarters a practical necessity, but doing so is also a great way to plug into the black community of your area. See Chapter 8 for tips on finding the right fit for your family.

## Consider a Cultural Camp

Cultural camps are offered by various organizations around the country. *Adoptive Families* magazine always maintains a current listing of camps during the summer and throughout the year. A few examples include Hands Around The World in Illinois, Colorado Heritage Camps, A Black Heritage Experience in Wisconsin, and Pact: An Adoption Alliance in California. While my family has not had the opportunity to participate in a cultural camp, I am told by members of our support group, Parenting Across Color, the experience is priceless for the entire family.

> *My oldest son declared himself*
> *cultural advisor of the family.*
> — *Bobbie Kerr, McKinney, TX; mother of four*

## Don't Be Color-Blind

To ignore your child's ethnicity is to deny the most obvious feature of your kiddo. While this was the recommended course of action for transracial parents many years ago, it is no longer recommended. According to a recent study at the University of Texas, racial profiling starts at a very early age.[1] University of Texas Professor of Psychology Dr. Becky Bigler, who supervised the study, reports, "We know the process starts very early in development. Many parents we meet say their child doesn't notice race yet and they are color-blind. They play with someone and don't even notice their race. We now know that's not true at all." University of Texas researcher Dr. Erin Pahlke studied 84 white mothers and their children, ages four and five, by having mothers read two books to their preschoolers. Both books featured issues of race. The results were clear that white parents tend not to discuss race, which is part of our white privilege. People of color are not as fortunate in being able to ignore the color of their skin. While we may see our children as miracles, the world will simply see them as black. Do your child a favor early on by acknowledging their ethnicity. Through this affirmation by the most important person in their life, you will lay the cornerstone of their cultural identity.

Talk about race with your children. Notice the differences and celebrate the likenesses. I recently met an African-American man who was adopted by a white family in the 1970s. He is now in his mid 30s and a father to his own children. This wonderful man has never been able to talk to his parents about their differences. The times he has tried to talk about race have ended in arguments and hurt feelings. How sad his parents can't truly know him for the man he is. The stumbling block in their relationship is race. Don't let this be your story. Acknowledge the pink elephant in the room! Your children know they are black. You know they are black. If you deny or avoid the obvious, your child will sense something is wrong and feel ashamed. I know hundreds of adoptive parents and I'm certain not one of them ever wants their child to feel ashamed. We adopted out of love. Now, let's live in love.

## Seven Common Transracial Parenting Mistakes

*Dr. Willie B. Garrett* [2]

Transracial adoption may present challenges that can lead to a rewarding family experience. Persons who live in a family where more than one culture is valued and practiced will have an advantage in adapting to our increasingly global society. Population projections indicate that by the year 2020 every person in the United States will live or work with persons of another background, and approximately half of all marriages will be bicultural or biracial.

Transracial adoptions are not a new phenomenon despite increased publicity over the past few years. Informal and formal transracial adoptions have occurred for centuries all around the world. However, misconceptions about transracial adoption persist. For example, current thinking suggests that to raise a child who can cope with prejudice and have a positive racial identity, parents must be of the same racial group. This is contrary to my own 20-year experience as a therapist and to reports I have received from other therapists. The vast majority of children we see who have identity and behavior problems are being raised by same-race parents and are living in their own cultural community. More than anything this suggests parenting is an art, not hard science.

Although I believe that being of the same race is helpful but not required to raise a child with a positive racial identity, as an African-American psychologist who specializes in psychotherapy with adoptive families, I have observed that parents of transracially adopted children commonly have problems related to the following seven issues.

## 1. Focusing Only on Racial/Cultural Issues

Openly acknowledging differences is important, or course, but too often parents only discuss differences. Parents must balance their acknowledgment of differences with their recognition of similarities, including shared likes, dislikes, common interests, personality traits, temperament, gender, spirituality, and elements of family culture, including shared beliefs, traditions, rituals, and celebrations. There are many universal mediums, such as music, that all groups share.

Bonding between parent and child is reinforced by similarities. While being of different races may seem to constitute a big difference, according to a study in *Discover* magazine, race accounts for less than one percent of the characteristics of a racial group. In that study, researchers compared physical characteristics among various racial groups and found that the statistical difference in any one characteristic (i.e., lip size, hair texture, finger prints, etc.,) was less than one percent.

## 2. Accepting Racism or Stereotypes as a Reason for Underachievement or Bad Behavior

Particularly when parents focus on differences, some transracially adopted children use racism or cultural expectations to explain poor choices they have made. For example, a child who feels he or she is being treated differently by a teacher may use that as an excuse for doing poorly in that teacher's class, or a child who wants an expensive athletic jersey or jacket with his or her favorite athlete's name on it may use racial stereotypes or issues of cultural acceptance to persuade parents that he or she needs the item.

In situations where a child is being treated differently, parents should intervene. However, the child must still be held accountable for his or her work and responsibilities. I am not aware of any culture that condones disrespectful behavior, swearing, smoking, etc., and while many groups across society wear athletic clothing, no culture describes wearing it as a cultural preference or characteristic. To assess the child's claim of disparate treatment, parents should consider the child's level of responsibility at home and apply this to school and other environments. The single most important factor is the child's character. Parents must first look at objective evidence (i.e., test scores, completed assignments, etc.) then proceed to assess subjective evidence (such as reports from other adults or kids and their child's complaints).

When the evidence confirms that your child has been responsible but has not been treated the same as other children, then you have disparate treatment, which is racism.

## 3. Overindulging the Child

Out of fear of being labeled inadequate, many parents of transracially adopted children tend to overreact to their child's wants and needs. While children should get all that they need for healthy growth and development, they shouldn't get everything they want. Many parents, however, provide excess gifts and toys, too many structured activities, or too much entertainment; or they over-respond to their child's every emotion. Children given too many of these extras often become self-centered and have difficulty coping with life's usual frustrations.

## 4. Allowing Others to Intrusively Touch or Violate the Child's Boundaries

Out of fear of disapproval, some parents refrain from telling others not to touch or excessively compliment their child. Some people experience anxiety when they encounter racial differences between a parent and child, and they overreact to mask their discomfort. Typically, such people react by touching the child's hair or repeatedly commenting on his or her attractiveness, responses they do not present to birth children. Children often report feeling "like a puppy" when this happens. Birth siblings report feeling ignored or unimportant. In such situations, parents must assertively but gently set limits, even if they offend the person giving the unwanted attention. Caucasian parents have reported to me that simply saying something like, "Thank you. I think all children are beautiful, but please do not touch my child's hair," or "Thank you, but I feel uncomfortable when people touch her hair," or "Sorry, but I don't allow anyone to touch her hair," works well. Children do not have the ability to stand up for themselves at such times.

## 5. Not Embracing Diversity

Transracially adopted children should have frequent exposure to people of various backgrounds to gain a sense that it is okay to be different. The family must become bicultural and practice at least some of the child's ethnic heritage. Celebrating Kwanzaa or sending the child to Korean camp once a year will not be sufficient exposure to develop a positive racial identity. The home must reflect ethnic symbols, and cultural education should be a frequent topic of family conversation and a frequent focus of family activities.

The cultural focus should be for the family's benefit, not for the child alone. Becoming bicultural means integrating at least one additional culture into the family's lifestyle and culture. If all family members receive a cultural education, the child will not feel different. Having at least one monthly family event (ethnic dinner, video, celebration, etc.) is helpful, but complement this with conversation several times a week (concepts such as attractiveness, success, and community need to be challenged and broadened in family conversation) and daily exposure through symbols around the house (e.g., books, art, etc.). Any time cultural education is focused on the child alone, it may become distancing and have a negative effect.

## 6. Not Challenging Racism

Racism today is less aggressive and tends to be "invisible" in the forms of attitude, voice tone, body language and posture, or institutional practices. Parents must be alert to disparate treatment and advocate on their child's behalf. Racism should be a family and community concern that is communicated as harmful to everyone.

## 7. Accepting Powerlessness

Out of fear of inadequacy, parents may adopt an attitude of powerlessness. They demonstrate this by second-guessing themselves and delaying timely parenting decisions. Small issues often become large, and indecisive debates become harmful to the marital and parent–child relationships. The child may also experience confusion and feel unsupported. All children need to believe their parents are in charge and know what's best for them.

Professionals continue to disagree on whether parent–child cultural identification or bonding is of prime importance in adoption. My opinion is that a healthy permanent family is superior to an institution or foster home in meeting a child's emotional needs. I encourage all transracial adoptive parents to accept their own cultural and racial identification as a parenting strength, and to put their energy into making the world a better place for us all to live in.

*Dr. Willie B. Garrett is an adoptive parent and licensed psychologist in St. Paul, Minn.*

# Chapter 4

## Love Is Not Enough

*Children are not casual guests in our home. They have been loaned to us temporarily for the purpose of loving them and instilling a foundation of values on which their future lives will be built.* — James Dobson

I have heard, on occasion, certain people refer to me as naïve. I have been told numerous times in my youth that I look fabulous in rose-colored glasses. And then there's the P word, my personal favorite. Yes, the P word was first used to describe my mother and has since be used to describe me on many occasions. The P word, of course, is Pollyanna. I don't always see the glass half full, but I usually do. I want to believe the very best of people and give them the benefit of the doubt whenever feelings are hurt. Hopefully seeing the best in other people will allow them to see the best in me. My mother says faith is the spiritual fruit growing in me and so when given a choice, I choose to see the good.

Making this choice is not always easy because I know too much. In my perfect world, there would be no hate, racism would not exist, children would be safe wherever they go, war would be a thing of the past, drugs would be as harmless as candy, poverty would be extinct, and love would be enough. If I had my way, love would pay the bills, mend the fences, and raise the children. Fortunately, or unfortunately depending on how you look at the situation, this world does exist and it's called Heaven. Until we get there, I think it is safe to say there are some concepts we must adopt as truth in order to do right by our kiddos.

Let's start with the fact that love is *not* enough to successfully raise a child. Yes, love is fundamentally necessary to parenting children when the goal is to create well-adjusted, self-assured, productive adults, but our children need more. If love were all it took, the foster care system would be empty and orphanages would be ghost towns. In the process of being adopted, our children's culture is taken away and love alone cannot replace what was lost. I believe it is my duty as a mother to provide every necessary tool to aid them in becoming whom God intended. A giant piece of that identity is wrapped up in culture.

Since I do not share their culture, I made a promise to each of my daughters that I will go to any length necessary to introduce them to elements of their African-American culture and heritage. Some days I do a phenomenal job and other days, not so well. That's okay because parenting is not a contest. There is no race or finish line. We do the best we can in the moment and pray our babies will forgive us for the rest.

> *You can never have too much culture or ever become*
> *too integrated in your home.*
> *— Susan Griffith; Jonestown, TX; mother of 12*

When Madison was three, we decided to enroll her in dance class. I had taken dance when I was a child and loved it. I was confident Madison would too. I searched our suburb for a dance school with a mix of white, brown, and black children. The last thing I wanted to do was force Madison to join another all-white team, our family being the first. I discovered the Joyce Willett School of Dance in East Austin near Madison's preschool, Mt. Sinai Christian Academy. The class included a few white girls, a few Hispanic girls, and a lot of black ones. This was it! I naïvely registered Maddie for a dance class at 9 a.m. on Saturday mornings, never taking into consideration that the dance school was 25 minutes away from our home! Ugh! Getting up early on a Saturday was never easy, but I loved watching Maddie dance and I thoroughly enjoyed sitting with the other mothers during class. This was a great way for me to connect with other moms and learn many things I didn't know. We talked about hair, we talked about clothes, and we talked about anything and everything that had to do with our babies. I learned so much from these women and felt such appreciation for being included in their conversations. Over the years, our kids grew up together and we grew closer. What a gift! This is what I mean when I say: Go to any length. Find the opportunities to put your child in the majority, regardless of where or when or how early. The prize is having a child who feels like a member of the pack.

I work hard to find ways to incorporate culture into our family. In doing so, I am helping my children build their racial identity. I want to fill their senses with affirming images of people of color. I want my children to know who they are and have pride in being that person.

According to Dr. Ruth McRoy's 1983 study, *Transracial and Inracial Adoptees: The Adolescent Years,*[1] in a survey of 30 adolescent black children adopted by white parents, only ten of them identified themselves as black; six said they were "mixed," and the rest tried to avoid a racial identity altogether by saying they were "human" or "American." Racial identity is paramount to creating a positive self-image. How do you want your son or daughter to self-identify?

Pick up Karen Beaumont's book, *I Like Myself!* and read it first to yourself and then to your kids. The book's snappy rhymes and charming illustrations model the positive messages we want our children to internalize. My girls love it as much as I do, even as they have no idea the deep impact these words have on their spirits.

In his online article on www.elev8.com, "Would You Adopt a Child of Another Race?" writer Stuart McDonald explains that our children need help in building a positive self-image and as parents, we need to be aware of the challenges associated with this effort. "It's crucial for children of color to understand that they are no less ... attractive just because they don't 'match' with those around them." McDonald states that white parents are bound to find it a challenge "to effectively affirm a child's appearance when they've never known the issues associated with creating a positive self-image" that differs from "the mainstream, Euro-centric image that America deems beautiful."

According to a study published in 2008 by the Evan B. Donaldson Adoption Institute,[2] parents of transracially adopted children are often unprepared to raise children who by virtue of their race are going to have to deal with difficult issues of identity and race as they grow up. But for all their lack of preparation for the role, most transracial adoptive parents I've met are willing to go to great lengths to raise a healthy child. Sometimes that means operating outside of your comfort zone in order to do what is right for your baby. Sometimes it means physically moving to a more diverse area in which your child can be surrounded by members of his own race. Sometimes it means simply opening your mind to the possibility there may be another side to the history lesson. I have faith in adoptive parents because I have seen ordinary people do extraordinary things for the love of a child.

When Madison entered the first grade, she began a time of intense self-awareness. She was painfully aware that most of the children in her class were pink like me. Crying to me before bed one night, she asked why there couldn't be more brown kids in her school. Let me just say that no matter how much you prepare to be a parent or an adoptive parent, nothing will cut you like a knife worse than listening to your child's painful experience at school that day. The emotion is intense and raw for you and the child. There is no time to reference a parenting book or call a friend. You go with your gut and pray it is enough. As I listened to Madison cry, I realized I couldn't change the racial makeup of her school, but I could bring together every brown face I could find.

I decided to form a Brown Beauties play group for Madison and McKenzie. I called every parent I knew in the neighborhood with a brown little girl. I even called some parents who lived outside of the neighborhood. We made a date to let the children play and play they did. Everyone had fun and my girls were in the majority. This was a great opportunity for me to connect with other moms, and especially brown moms. We talked about hair, school, Justin Bieber, and anything else that held the interest of our daughters. I also discovered African-American mothers in my neighborhood were also looking for cultural opportunities for their children. The Brown Beauties group met everyone's needs. And I hope these children will always be friends who can depend on each other when times are tough in middle school and beyond.

Love is not enough to successfully raise a child because there are forces at play in this world over which we have no control and little influence. As a Type A white woman, I hate admitting this. In my mind, I am a force of nature. I am a change-it, get-it, make-it-happen kind of girl. Since I can't change certain things, it helps to be aware of their existence. In opening our own eyes, perhaps we can enlighten other people, which might be enough to someday change the world.

# Chapter 5

## White Privilege

*If you bungle raising your children, I don't think whatever else you do matters much.* — Jacqueline Kennedy Onassis

Racism is alive and well in the United States of America. I witnessed it on a daily basis as a young person growing up in Mississippi. I see evidence of racism on the news and read about it in the paper. I am more likely to experience racism when I am with my children. Our country was built on the idea that white skin is better than dark skin, which would make white people better than black people. This concept is commonly referred to as white privilege. Ora Houston with St. James Episcopal Church explained white privilege to me during a Parenting Across Color meeting many years ago. I was crushed. I did not want her to be right, but I knew in my heart she was. White privilege is the undeserved advantages I am automatically given based on my skin color. And there is evidence of it everywhere.

The first time I recognized white privilege was on Christmas Eve, 2003. We were expecting people over for the holiday and were frantically cooking and cleaning when the vacuum cleaner died. I drove to Fry's Electronics hoping to quickly buy a new one. I stood in front of what seemed like hundreds of vacuums trying to decide which one was right for me. I had no idea there were so many choices. A young salesman was anxious to sell one to me, but I couldn't decide which one. In his excitement to make a sale, he began to annoy me. I needed a few minutes of quiet contemplation. Basically, I needed him to leave me alone. As I stood there reading about the bells and whistles of this one and that one, I saw a middle-aged black woman standing on the same aisle with her selection already made.

Why wasn't he complimenting her choice? Why wasn't he carrying her box to the register? Why wasn't he ringing up her sale? Why wasn't he talking to this woman as enthusiastically as he was bugging, I mean talking to, me since she was ready to buy a vacuum cleaner? I will tell you why. She was black and I am white. This young salesman assumed that I had bundles of cash in my pocket and impeccable credit. In fact, neither of these assumptions was true. More than likely, the other woman had a higher bank balance than I did, but the assumption was, white people have money. White privilege strikes again.

As I said before, I didn't want to believe white privilege exists. Privately, I tried to blow holes in the theory in order to make myself feel better. The guilt of knowing I was receiving undeserved, unsolicited benefits simply because of my skin color was eating me alive.

What could I do about it? Nothing.

How could I change it? I can't.

How could I give those advantages to my children rather than keep them for myself? Not possible.

Recognizing and acknowledging white privilege is vitally important to successfully parenting a child of a different race. Work your way through the guilt and then get on with the job of raising your baby. Your children are not served by your guilt. You can't change it. The best thing you can do is to be aware and confront the assumptions whenever possible.

White privilege has to be the largest unspoken agreement within our country. We are conditioned to believe white is better, richer, cleaner, and more desirable. In movies, the good guys are dressed in white while the bad guys are dressed in black. Our society convinces every member that white is better, including my brown babies. The first time you hear your son tell you he wants to have white skin like yours or your daughter wants straight hair like yours, it just might break your heart. I am already pointing out to Madison the irony of white people spending tremendous amounts of money to darken their skin every summer at the risk of their own health or financial well-being, and yet so many minorities want to appear white to gain the privileges white skin brings.

White privilege is a commonly held belief that is perpetuated generation after generation. My children see it. I see it. Perhaps the beauty and courage of families like ours will someday be the catalyst to change this system of racism in our country. It took some time for me to accept the concept, but once I did, I saw it everywhere. Dr. Peggy McIntosh of Wellesley College wrote an incredible article on White Privilege, making the concept undeniably real. The article is entitled *Unpacking the Invisible Knapsack* and I encourage every parent to locate it on the internet and read. As a matter of fact, print a copy to refer to every now and then. It will change the way you see the world forever.

# Chapter 6

## Role Models

*The child must know that he is a miracle, that since the beginning of the world there hasn't been, and until the end of the world there will not be, another child like him.*
— Pablo Casals

When I first became a mother to a child of a different race, I was terrified of black women. Seriously. I avoided black women in the grocery store, in parking lots, everywhere! My worst fear involved a black woman grabbing my baby from my arms and telling me I wasn't fit to parent this child. I now see that this nightmare scenario had more to do with my own insecurities as a new parent than with reality.

Much to my surprise, black women embraced us when I finally let my guard, or personal insecurities, down. It has been my experience that people will surprise you when given the chance. Over the years, many black women have struck up conversation with me about my children. The conversations often go like this:

"Oh, my goodness, she's so pretty!" says Mrs. Black-Stranger.

"Thank you," I beam.

"What's her name?" she inquires.

"Madison," I reply.

"Oh that's pretty! How old is she?"

And then one of two things will happen at this point. Mrs. Black-Stranger will either compliment my daughter's hair or make a recommendation on how I should do her hair. Please make a mental note that you are in no way required to follow every recommendation made to you regarding your daughter's hair. If you try, you'll end up chasing your tail like a dog.

> *I do not live in a racially diverse area, but it is getting better. My first concern when I adopted was how the community would react to our family, but I was pleasantly surprised how well the community responded. I have a difficult time finding hair care products and hairstylists within 30 miles of our home. I also have a hard time finding resources for our family. There are three black families in our church. I sometimes feel predatory finding black families for play dates or to make new friends.*
> — *Sandra Nosik, Caldwell, ID; mother of one*

As my love for my daughter grew, so my eyes grew wider and my walls shrank. More often than not, I am embraced by the black community while members of my own white community look at me as if I have arrived from Mars when they see me out and about with my children. What I now realize is how much I need this black community in order to successfully raise my children. This community is where I find potential role models. I am relying on the strength of this community to teach my daughters how to be one of them because I will only hold those little hands for a few years before they must find their place in their cultural community. While I see each daughter as a miracle from God, the world sees them as little black girls. Someday the world will see them as black women, but the bigger question is, how will they see themselves?

When I was a little girl, I wanted to be a dancer. I loved to dance! I took tap, ballet, and jazz classes every week. I was a die-hard fan of the television show *Solid Gold* and I entered every talent show I found. Looking back, I don't think I was a very good dancer, but I loved dancing.

My dad's sister, Spence, is a professional dancer. When I was a child, she was dancing on Broadway and living my dream. I heard the story over and over again about how she left college to follow her heart by making it as a dancer in New York City. As you know, you can make it anywhere if you can make it in New York City.

Spence came to visit when I was in the third grade and agreed to perform for my dance class. My mother thought Spence didn't look well as she waited to perform for a group of eight- and nine-year-old kids. When Mom asked if she was okay, Spence told her she was suffering from severe stage fright. Mom laughed and said, "They are just kids, Spence! Anything you do will be amazing!"

Spence explained, "Kids are painfully honest and I can see their faces! I'm scared to death!"

As a child, Spence was my role model. I wanted to be Spence, or rather a dancer, when I grew up. Thirty years later and I still have every poster of every show in which she was cast. I cannot bring myself to get rid of them because they were such a treasured part of my childhood. While my parents served as wonderful role models to me as parents, Christians, Scout leaders, and such, they could not show me how to be what they were not.

In the same way, I cannot show my children how to be what I am not and one thing I am not is black. I have never been black and I never will be. I simply do not have those life lessons to pass on to my daughters. We require role models to accomplish this task. I used to feel guilty for not having everything my children need in order to grow up to be successful adults. I didn't like the feeling of needing other adults to help me raise my children until I considered how my mother must have felt when I found a role model in my aunt. Do you think my mother was jealous or resentful that she could not fill my every need? Do you think she longed to be a Broadway dancer? No! My mother could not be for me what she was not herself. It takes a village!

> *I want role models for my sons. I want real men to show my boys what it looks like to be a man living at home, raising kids and loving their wives.*
> *— Jennifer Danvers, Taylor, TX; mother of three*

So who will your children's role models be? Of course, there will be the role models who show them how to be a baseball player, or dancer, or firefighter, or whatever your child wants to be. Have you considered who will show them how to be black in America? Let's consider the available options of role models.

For the first time in the history of our country, we can list the President of the United States as a realistic role model for our children. I remember well the night President Obama was elected. I watched with tears in my eyes as crowds gathered in Chicago to celebrate this moment in history. I dragged Madison and McKenzie from their beds to have them watch the celebration. I tried to explain how many doors this one event had opened for them. Regardless of your political opinions, the election of a black man to the highest office of our country is an amazing accomplishment. We have come a long way in electing people of color to political office. We still have more work to do and wouldn't it be amazing if one of our children someday joins this category of powerful black political figures, like Condoleezza Rice, Barbara Jordan, Colin Powell, Governor David Patterson, and countless others.

Other role models for our children are musicians. These often highly publicized media figures tell the story of their personal life through music. Some of the stories they tell are not the wholesome life experiences I want for my children! Do I want Lil' Kim to teach my daughters how to be black in America? No. Do I want my children to adopt the world view of Ludacris or Snoop Dog? No. While I know my children will more than likely be influenced by these musicians and many others as they enter their teen years, for now, I want to be the one who chooses the people who show them how to be a member of their cultural community.

The best role models for my daughters are the parents of their friends, their coaches, their teachers, and our neighbors. These are the people with whom I have things in common. Sometimes I feel like a stalker of black mothers. Don't laugh; I am always looking for new friends and I have no problem striking up a conversation with a total stranger in hopes of benefitting my children through our friendship. For example, at Madison's seventh birthday party recently, I met the mother of Madison's friend Janae. Both Janae and her mother are black. I immediately connected with the mother and thought what great friends we could be. What a wonderful surprise it was to learn that Janae is also adopted. Janae is now part of our Brown Beauties playgroup and it makes me happy to see my children spend time with Janae's family. Not only did my reaching out to another parent help bridge the gap between my pink world and the elusive brown world, we discovered an additional connection that would be incredibly beneficial to my brown babies. Never be afraid to reach out of your comfort zone. You may be surprised by the response.

McKenzie was recently asked to join the invitational team of the school where she currently takes gymnastics. Of course, I was thrilled. In a split second I saw McKenzie standing on the podium at the 2022 Summer Olympics as the gold medal is hung around her neck and the national anthem plays! McKenzie loves gymnastics and I am pleased to find an activity she enjoys this much. It was only a year ago that we enrolled her in soccer at the YMCA only to watch her spend most of each practice lying in the grass picking flowers and talking with other kids. Soccer clearly was not her calling, so I wasn't likely to find role models on the soccer field.

Upon receiving the letter of invitation for the gymnastics team, my first concern was the commitment of time and finances, since McKenzie is just four years old. Then I attended an informational meeting for parents and, much to my delight, discovered the lead coach is black! Here was a great role model for McKenzie and a big score for my family! Coach Chris has been involved in gymnastics for 30 years and her commitment to children is admirable. I was convinced in the meeting this was the right thing to do for McKenzie given her love of the sport and the minimal increase of time and finances to join the team at this early age. Of course, having Coach Chris tell me McKenzie is something special and has true talent helped make the decision easy.

In addition to finding positive individual role models, also consider the environment in which you live. In 2007, we adopted McKenzie and moved my travel business to our home. Our 1500 square foot home was on the verge of exploding with two young children, two golden retrievers, two parents, and one business. We began the search for a larger home in the same suburb of Austin and found the house of our dreams in August. This house had everything we could ever want in a home and was nestled at the end of a small cul-de-sac. Our dream home was light years away from our budget, but somehow the stars aligned, serious negotiations took place, and we are now the proud owners of a home in which I plan to live until I die.

Making the deal even sweeter were the neighbors. There are seven houses on our cul-de-sac. There is an African-American family in one house, an interracial (black–white) family in another, an Asian family, a Hispanic family, two white families, and our transracial family with three African-American children. It was important to us for our children to see upper middle-class African-American families living right next door. Our neighbors are wonderful role models for our children and I am on constant patrol for other black families in the neighborhood. I need to know them! I want to know them! My children need to know them! Don't be afraid to stick out your neck, or your hand of friendship, if in doing so you find a way to benefit your children. I don't think it is possible for anyone to have a life that is too full or to have too many friends. Make the connection. Build the bridge of friendship for your child to cross into his or her own cultural community. These people may not be as personally influential as a coach or teacher, but believe me, it makes a difference in the view your child will have of how they fit into the world.

In December 2009, Disney released *The Princess and the Frog.* This was Disney's first black princess and it was a big deal in our house. I first read about the making of this movie in 2005 when several Mississippi friends emailed a story from the newspaper about a new Disney movie with a black princess named Maddie. Well, I was ecstatic since I had my very own Princess Maddie living down the hall. While I was disappointed to learn the main character's name was changed from Maddie to Tiana, I was thrilled to have my children see a fairy-tale princess on the big screen who shares their skin color.

My girls and I were so excited for the movie to premiere that we made a plan to invite our brown princess friends to join us at the theater on opening night wearing their favorite princess costumes. Madison and McKenzie were decked out in their finest dress-up costumes, complete with plastic jewelry, when we made our way to the theater. I had purchased our tickets earlier in the day so the royal gathering of little ladies could bypass any lines in the cold. We took lots of pictures in the lobby of the theater and were the envy of many other children. I honestly think I was more excited than the children! We had a wonderful time watching the movie and sharing popcorn. Tiana was beautiful, as we knew she would be, and the other characters were fabulous.

That Christmas, Santa brought Madison and McKenzie *Princess and the Frog* sheets, nightgowns, notebooks, hair bows, and anything else he could find! It isn't every day that my children get to see a positive role model on the big screen who speaks in terms they understand. Thank you, Disney!

Every child needs a role model. Make sure you have a hand in picking your child's cultural role models at an early age. These people will hold a great deal of power in the life of your child and their influence is priceless. Don't fool yourself into thinking you can do it all, because no one can. Every parent needs help. Every child needs a village. The white parents of black children require reinforcements and that is okay.

# Notable African-Americans

There are many great role models out there for our black children to admire and emulate. It's important for you to educate yourself about their accomplishments and find ways to introduce the ones you most admire to your kids. Here is a selection to get you started. Check out the website www.factmonster.com for short biographies of many of these notable African-Americans or look at www.wikipedia.org for more detailed bios. And remember, keeping a mix of figures in the media and figures in your neighborhood as role models creates a great balance.

## Sports Heroes

Muhammad Ali, Kobe Bryant, Dominique Dawes, Julius "Dr. J" Erving, Florence Griffith-Joyner, Shaquille O'Neal, Serena and Venus Williams, Dennis Rodman, Tiger Woods, Sheryl Swoopes

## Actors

Morgan Freeman, Tyra Banks, Samuel L. Jackson, Bill Cosby, Queen Latifah, Will and Jada Pinkett-Smith, Eddie Murphy, Eartha Kitt, Denzel Washington, Pam Grier

## Musicians

Brandy, Dr. Dre, Whitney Houston, Ray Charles, Ella Fitzgerald, Dizzy Gillespie, Jay-Z, Lauryn Hill, Billie Holiday, Usher

## Political Figures

Barack Obama, Colin Powell, Condoleezza Rice, Barbara Jordan, Martin Luther King, Jr., Thurgood Marshall, Sojourner Truth, Mary Bethune, Jesse Jackson, Shirley Chisholm

## Writers

Maya Angelou, W.E.B. Du Bois, Terry McMillan, Alice Walker, Alex Haley, Langston Hughes, Leonard Pitts, Jr., Zora Neale Hurston, Toni Morrison, Ernest Gaines

# Chapter 7

## Honor the Spirit

*Loving a child is a circular business ... the more you give, the
more you get; the more you get, the more you give.*
— Penelope Leach

Black, white, adopted or not, children are born to be the people God
intends them to be and not necessarily what we, their parents, want
them to be. It would be nice if children would do and be extensions of
us. Perhaps we would get along better. On the other hand, how boring
would life be if we were all the same? I want my daughters to be more
than me, better than me. I have always loved the scene from the book
and movie, *The Divine Secrets of the Ya-Ya Sisterhood*, by Rebecca
Wells, when the mother tells her daughter, "And then it dawned on
me. All those years that I prayed, that I begged on my hands and
knees, for God to make me more, give me more, make me better, make
me stronger, make me saner, make all my dreams come true. I finally
got the answer: You. Right there in one person, all I'd ever wanted to
be or do. And there you are." In seeing our children for who they are,
we honor their spirits.

When our children are infants, it is easy to become consumed
with caring for their physical needs because there are so many of them.
Babies have to be fed, bathed, dressed, diapered, and much more every
single day. All of those physical needs come with a lot of stuff. Now
that our family is complete, we are having a garage sale to pass along
some of that stuff to parents who need it. I am amazed when I see the
stack in our garage with two highchairs, multiple car seats, a double
stroller, a single stroller, a baby bathtub, boxes and boxes of clothes,
and the list goes on and on! Our children are completely helpless as
babies and their physical care consumes us for the first two years of
their life. We reach this two-year mark exhausted, dazed, and weary.

Thankfully, our kids become more independent as they grow. My
older children can already do many things for themselves, like
dressing and bathing, that my youngest still needs me to do for her.

They can even contribute to the household through chores, making it easier to meet the physical needs of our family. During this time of increased independence, personalities begin to emerge. In our family, Morgan, the youngest, is the prankster. She likes to hide from her sisters and then jump from behind furniture or out from corners to surprise them. Morgan will grab whatever you are using at the moment and run away with it, laughing the whole time. She keeps our family in stitches with her laughter and pranks. These are the ways she shows us her spirit.

The spirit of our children is found deep within and, I believe, is connected to the soul. It is the spirit that distinguishes one body from another, making each of us unique. To witness my children's spirit is to see who they are on the inside, the essence of the child. And while it is true we are each the same color on the inside of our physical bodies, race and culture are a vital part of the spirit of a person. It is who we are. Our bodies are like a lamp, coming in a variety of shapes and sizes. Our spirit is the light beneath the lampshade, shining brightly and clearly, illuminating the style of the lamp.

As new parents, it is easy to become caught up in meeting the physical needs of our babies and forget about their spirit. The body is highly demanding, requiring constant attention that is usually audible. The spirit of a new life is often quiet and easy to miss. Do you remember the rock musical *Tommy,* by The Who? There is a scene in which the doctor is telling the parents there is no hope their child Tommy will ever be normal, as Tommy sings, "See me, feel me, touch me, heal me." Isn't this what every human spirit cries to the world? If my daughter's spirit could speak to me directly, I believe it would sound like this.

"*See me.* See me for who I am. I am not you. I am different from you. I am black. Celebrate our likenesses and acknowledge, no, *embrace*, our differences.

"*Feel me.* Feel my brown skin as soft as velvet. Feel the thickness of my skin, made this way from generations of oppression. My skin can be dry and cracked with a fierce thirst for moisture, but when you love my skin and quench its thirst, it is soft and supple and shiny like the moon.

"*Touch me.* Touch my curly coarse hair and do not be afraid, for my hair is part of who I am and it cannot hurt you. It can merely intimidate you for as long as you let it. My hair is capable of things yours can never do. My hair is like the clay on a potter's wheel, capable of being shaped and styled into beautiful creations of art. My hair is a thing of beauty to be admired and revered.

"*Heal me.* I am small and young yet I have sustained the greatest loss ever known to humankind for I have lost my birth mother. Good or bad, right or wrong, she was all I had and now she is gone. Before I was ever placed in your arms, my heart was broken into a thousand pieces because the only voice, the only touch, the only heartbeat I have ever known has gone away. I will spend the rest of my life reconciling this loss and I will need your help. My pain has nothing to do with you because you did not cause it. When I work to ease the hurt, do not feel rejected because this is merely my effort to feel whole again. You cannot heal me. That is my job. Just know that healing is required from the very start of my life. Accept me, love me, adore me, see me, and let me be the person I was born to be."

I take the business of honoring my children's spirits seriously because our spirit is the essence of who we are as people. When I was a child, I thought the women who worked in the school cafeteria were sisters, which totally confused my mother when I mentioned the family affair taking place in the lunchroom. I am embarrassed to admit that I believed these women were sisters because all of them were black. As a child, I could only see the color of their skin and I lumped them together as being part of one another because of this one similarity. These hard-working women were more than the color of their skin. They each had a spirit, making them unique in a multitude of ways. My children are the same way. Yes, they are black, but they are far more than the color of their skin.

I believe there are three major components to the spirit of my children. I want them to always know they are members of an incredible community of culture and heritage that I do not happen to share but completely embrace. I want them to know how much they are loved and that through this love, they were adopted into this family. And I want them to know they are normal sexual beings like everyone else. I remember the day my mother told me about the birds and the bees. She was making a salad in the kitchen when I was in the third grade. She told me how babies are made and in my mind, this was the sole reason that sex took place. I remember my dad walking into the kitchen while we were talking and turning on his heel to promptly leave the room. I never want Madison to remember what I was doing or what I was wearing the day she realized I am white and she is black. One of the many goals of my parenting is to have open, ongoing conversations with each of my children about race, sex, and adoption in order to embrace the whole person.

## Embrace the Similarities

My partner, Kim, has the flattest feet I have ever known anyone to have. I marvel at the way her foot completely meets the floor, whereas I have the tallest arches of anyone I know. Maybe the height of my arches is making up for my short stature. Madison was young when we realized how flat her feet were going to be and we began commenting on this often. We would tell her, "Your feet are just like Mama's!" This eventually led to observations like, "Your eyes are just as brown as Mommy's!"

When Madison was still in preschool, we were told she was bossy. I laughed out loud, thinking, "She can barely walk, how is she bossy?" As I was thinking aloud about this, Kim was looking at me with an intensity that could only mean, "This is *your* child." At seven years old, Madison is outgoing, charming, and tremendously funny. She is a natural leader and a dedicated organizer. She likes to write stories and sing in the car with me at top volume. We have many traits in common, to say the very least. Madison is also athletic and competitive like Kim.

McKenzie was the oldest child we adopted, coming home to us at close to 16 months. If I didn't know for certain she was born from another mother, I would swear she is my flesh and blood. We are both emotional creatures and very loud. We love to laugh and entertain. McKenzie has been obsessed with books since she came to us and I too am a lover of print. She is physically strong with an athlete's body and she is stubborn. These are a few areas of common ground she shares with Kim.

Morgan is fondly called "Hoss" in our family. While Madison is the dancer and McKenzie the gymnast, I feel certain Morgan will be the star hockey or peewee football player of the family. She is rough and tough with an infectious laugh, just like Kim. Morgan knows no fear. Whether Morgan is fearlessly jumping off the back of the couch or standing in the middle of the dining table entertaining the whole family, she and Kim share many traits. Morgan also loves to read and to snuggle, just like me. She is outgoing and friendly to everyone, telling every person we pass in Walmart, "Hi!"

As an only child for more than four years, Madison, as I am sure you can tell, has served as a guinea pig as we learned to be parents. I played the same role for my parents as the oldest child. I am sure I have made countless mistakes in her upbringing that I will later pay for when she lies on a therapist's couch someday. Our second child McKenzie has been the catalyst for great personal growth during the last three years. In recognizing how alike we are, I have the opportunity to examine why I do and say certain things and respond to life in certain ways. It has been like looking in the mirror. Morgan came into my life unexpectedly when I was working horrific hours in an attempt to save our family business. I was burned out and worn out. And then Morgan was born. Her arrival changed my entire life, reordering my priorities in a split second. I am profoundly thankful for each daughter and I do my best to accept on a daily basis the individuals they are becoming.

Having been in the trenches of parenthood for over seven years now, I can already tell you, with certainty: my children have more in common with their parents than they have differences. The differences may be mighty, don't misunderstand, but as a family, we share much of who we are with our children. Dance with joy on the common ground. Celebrate it.

## Embrace the Differences

"Yes, I am pink and you are brown. This is not something you are imagining."

Children generally begin to pick up on the differences in skin color around age three. We were expecting a giant Aha moment from Madison when she turned three, but that is not what happened. In fact, there was nothing giant about her recognizing the profound difference between us. One day, while sitting on the couch reading a book, she said to me, "My skin is darker than yours." I agreed with her. I let her steer the conversation from there but very little else was said. Over the years, of course, the conversations became more detailed as we later discussed skin pigment, shades of light and dark, and why our skin is different. As our family grew, Madison expressed pleasure in announcing the brown people now outnumber the pink ones in our family.

Madison attended preschool in a predominantly black environment. The night before kindergarten started, I asked her how she would answer any questions from her new friends in her new class at her new school about the difference in our skin color.

"They won't ask," she assured me.

"Let's pretend they did ask. What will you say?"

"They won't ask, Mommy."

"Just pretend they did ask. How will you answer?" I pressed her.

Exasperated, Madison shouted, "I'll just tell them I am brown and you are pink and that is the way I was born and that's just the way our family is! Okay?"

"That will do just fine," I said quietly.

At five years old, Madison understood we were different and she also understood we were a family. Somehow we prepared her to face the questions that would eventually come in kindergarten. I left her the next day in her new classroom, confident in knowing Madison is sure of who she is.

Kindergarten was a positive wonderful experience with very few racial hiccups. Fast-forward to the first grade and I was totally unprepared for the gut-wrenching pain Madison's heightened sense of self-awareness would bring to our family.

I find myself on the staircase in our home with Madison in meltdown mode. She won't let me hold her. She is saying things like, "We're not a real family because we're not all brown! Only my sisters are my family." She calls herself dumb and a brat. My heart is breaking and I am struggling with what to do in this moment on the stairs while one of the loves of my life cries heartbroken tears. And then I hear the voice of Dr. Steve of the Austin Attachment and Counseling Center telling me: "Find the place of agreement."

I close my mouth and just listen to what Madison says. I respond quietly.

"That must feel awful."

"You must feel very lonely."

"How sad."

And suddenly Madison is crawling into my lap. She is letting me touch her, hold her. I tell her it is okay to be sad. I tell her we'll just sit here and be sad together for as long as it takes. We sit together for a couple of minutes until she jumps out of my lap and returns with possibly the longest children's book ever written and hands it to me. I read every word.

The meltdown is over. It ended as quickly as it started. We survived. Dr. Steve, in fact, does know what he is talking about and I will never again approach an emotional situation the way I used to.

I don't know when the next meltdown will happen. I don't know where we will be or who will be watching, but I do know my mouth will stay closed more than it is open. I have never been black and I never will be. I cannot begin to know what it feels like to lose my birth mother, look different from everyone else, and feel alone in a sea of pink people. The only thing I can do is honor her spirit by letting her cry, letting her scream, letting her be mad. I can handle it. So can Madison. We don't have all the answers or understand the mysteries of the human condition, but I am willing to learn them with her no matter what it takes because I love her, no matter what.

## Introduce Culture

One of the greatest days of my life was the day Madison was baptized. We invited every friend and relative to join us for a weekend of revelry to celebrate Madison's baptism. On Saturday night, we held a party in a private room at the library. We ate fabulous Texas barbeque, visited with old friends, and opened presents. I was on cloud nine! I don't think my feet ever touched the ground the entire weekend. I reveled in my motherhood and celebrated the blessing of my daughter.

The next morning, Kim and I walked into our church with over 40 friends and family to be part of our daughter's baptism. I am sure it looked like a parade with Madison leading the way! Midway through the service, our family was called to the altar and we were surrounded by godparents and family. Our minister, Rev. Ken Martin, held Madison in his arms and I had a chance to see her clearly for the first time that weekend. She was dressed in a beautiful white gown and around her neck hung a stole made of kente cloth that was made for this occasion by a member of the church. In this one image was the tradition from our white Christian culture of the baptism gown combined with the kente cloth stole of West African origin. Through our daughter, the two cultures were merged.

Each of my children has worn this stole during their baptismal ceremonies and I cherish this piece of cloth by keeping it wrapped and stored carefully away for when my grandchildren are someday baptized. Each daughter has her own baptism gown to pass on to her own children in the tradition of our families of origin. I like to think we have taken extra care to honor our children's spirits by introducing their culture into the ceremonies of our own heritage.

## Accept the Child for Who They Are

I am sure birth parents can tell you a variety of stories about the ways in which their biological children are totally different from themselves. Since I am not a birth parent, I can only tell you about my experiences as an adoptive parent. Regardless of whether or not your children are adopted, our kids are not always just like us. McKenzie, for example, is different from her sisters in a few ways that stand out in our family on a regular basis. She is loud, like me. She is a picky eater. She is more emotional than the other two. I can become irritated by her choice of volume, or frustrated with her eating habits, or exhausted from emotional outbursts. Like it or not, this is who McKenzie is. I cannot change her. I can only accept her as the person God created and sent to me. Constantly correcting her would be a futile attempt to change her. And since I can only control myself, I choose to accept McKenzie just as she is. In doing so, I honor her spirit.

## A Transracially Adopted Child's Bill of Rights

*Adapted by Liza Steinberg Triggs from* "A Bill of Rights for Mixed Folks," *by Marilyn Dramé* [1]

- Every child is entitled to love and full membership in her family.
- Every child is entitled to have his culture embraced and valued.
- Every child is entitled to parents who know that this is a race-conscious society.
- Every child is entitled to parents who know that she will experience life differently than they do.
- Every child is entitled to parents who are not looking to "save" him or to improve the world.
- Every child is entitled to parents who know that being in a family doesn't depend on "matching."
- Every child is entitled to parents who know that transracial adoption changes the family forever.
- Every child is entitled to be accepted by extended family members.

- Every child is entitled to parents who know that, if they are white, they benefit from racism.
- Every child is entitled to parents who know that they can't transmit the child's birth culture if it is not their own.
- Every child is entitled to have items at home that are made for and by people of his race.
- Every child is entitled to opportunities to make friends with people of her race or ethnicity.
- Every child is entitled to daily opportunities of positive experiences with his birth culture.
- Every child is entitled to build racial pride within her own home, school, and neighborhood.
- Every child is entitled to have many opportunities to connect with adults of the child's race.
- Every child is entitled to parents who accept, understand, and empathize with her culture.
- Every child is entitled to learn survival, problem-solving, and coping skills in a context of racial pride.
- Every child is entitled to take pride in the development of a dual identity and a multicultural/multiracial perspective on life.
- Every child is entitled to find his multiculturalism to be an asset and to conclude, "I've got the best of both worlds."

# Chapter 8

## It's All About the Hair

*Parents are often so busy with the physical rearing of children*
*that they miss the glory of parenthood, just as the grandeur of*
*the trees is lost when raking leaves.* — Marcelene Cox

I clearly remember receiving the call announcing the arrival of my daughter Madison. I was at work with a client at my desk when I received the news. The baby was ten days old, the social worker told me. She was born prematurely, had a few health concerns and, oh yeah, she's black.

Black? Hmmm. I hadn't considered this possibility. I just wanted a baby.

God bless my client, a beautiful black woman in her late 20s, who watched me flip-flop between laughter and tears. In between hanging up the phone and dashing out the door, the only question I verbalized was, "What will I do with her hair?" My young yet very wise client replied, "Calm down. More than likely, she won't have any yet."

I was not alone in fearing hair care for black children. I have spoken with dozens of white parents over the years whose list of top five concerns about raising a black child includes hair. And we are absolutely justified in our fear and apprehension. Hair is no small matter in the African-American community. It's all about the hair.

Attention, white people:

- Your child's hair is different from your own.
- You will *not* automatically know how to care for his or her hair.
- Caring for your child's hair is far more involved than caring for your own.
- It is okay to ask for help while you learn.
- The *worst* mistake you can make is to treat your child's hair as if it were Caucasian hair.

In the black community, hair is a creative expression of cultural pride and occupies a special place in black culture. As Ayana Byrd and Lori Tharps explain in their book *Hair Story: Untangling the Roots of Black Hair in America,* "From day one, black children are indoctrinated into the intricate culture of hair. Vocabulary words like *grease, kitchen* (the hair at the nape of the neck…), and *touch-up* are ones a black child hears at a very early age and needs to learn in order to fully participate in the black hair lifestyle. Phrases like *nappy-headed* … and *turn back* … are absorbed into the growing lexicon of a young black mind. Before a black child is even born, relatives speculate over the texture of [their] hair … and the loaded adjectives 'good' and 'bad' are already in the air."

This is especially true for little girls. I have a creative freedom with my children's hair that I would never have known had I adopted a child who looks like me. Not only do my children feel proud when their hair looks beautiful, but I feel a sense of pride in my abilities as a mother. I am validated as a mother by members of the black community when they see the success of my hairstyling efforts and the love this shows for my children. When I was a little girl, there were three hairstyles available to me: one ponytail, two ponytails, or French braids. Not true for my daughters! They can have as many ponytails as they want! My children's hair can be shaped and sculpted into a multitude of styles, making me feel like a hair artist. My daughters stand taller when their hair is freshly combed and neatly styled. When we look good, we feel good. And when we feel good, we do good things. As parents, we want the best for our children and the first step in that right direction is to ensure they feel good about themselves. Hair grooming is an absolute necessity when raising a black child.

It is also a tremendous undertaking to learn the craft of hair combing. If you are anything like me, it is easy to become overwhelmed when shopping for shampoo. Have you ever noticed the sheer number of options on the shampoo aisle at the store? There are choices for color-treated hair, oily hair, dry hair, and combination hair. There are price ranges for every budget. Do you smell them too? As many options as there are for our own hair, there are just as many for our children's hair. There are products for dry hair, color-treated hair, relaxed hair and natural hair. There are products for braided hair, extensions, and the scalp. You can get a different opinion from every African-American adult you meet on how to care for, style, and maintain your child's hair. It is easy to feel confused about who and what to believe because you want the very best for your kiddo. Don't beat yourself up — we all feel this way at some point. As white parents, we don't have a natural reference point for how to care for our children's hair. And that's okay, because we can learn.

My best suggestion is to accept advice whenever it is offered until you know enough to decipher what is good and what isn't. I once had a grandmotherly figure in Walmart tell me I should put Crisco in Madison's hair. Fortunately, I can recognize an old wives' tale from 20 paces and thanked her graciously for the advice. Bless her, she meant well.

Do not underestimate the role hair plays in raising a child of a different race. I was 29 years old when Madison was born and had never touched the hair of a black person. Even though I grew up in South Mississippi where white children are the minority in public schools, I had no idea how coarse, curly, or fragile my daughter's hair would be. Nothing in my life experience equipped me to care for Madison's hair.

So, where is a white girl to go for help? The answer: day care! I turned to Madison's caregivers, the black teachers in her day care, and asked them for help. I stayed after school to practice with them. We would comb and part and tie tiny rubber bands.

I also paid attention to other children her age. I asked questions of their mothers. A mom will never turn you down for advice when you praise the appearance of her child. At home, I would experiment, developing styles on my own. Not every day-care provider is willing to guide you through the hair process. You may need to explore asking a good friend for a hair session, making an appointment with a stylist, attending a class offered through an adoption support group or child welfare agency, or buying a video and some good books. It is important to learn the process of combing hair early in the game because it is a daily necessity.

As a white mother, it seemed cruel to put Madison through a process that often hurt. It upset me to struggle to make her sit still, but eventually I won. White mothers of black children often confess to me they can't or won't put their daughter through the ordeal of combing and styling hair. "It is just too upsetting to both of us," is what I often hear. However, without the process, black hair becomes tangled and dry patches develop on the scalp that cause terrible itching. The itching leads to open sores, which is embarrassing and a health hazard. The same parents who are unwilling to style their child's hair properly often find themselves uncomfortable interacting with black families because they know the hair doesn't look good. This is the last thing you want! What we are doing as parents is preparing our children for a lifetime of high maintenance hair. It isn't optional — hair must be groomed. Parents must find a way to complete the process. In my home, a happy medium was found when I allowed Madison to comb my hair after I finished her hair. It wasn't pretty, but it worked.

Hair grooming is a fact of life for all black children. The sooner they accept it and grow accustomed to the process, the easier it will be for everyone. And this is what I believe gets a white lady's foot in the door of the black community. At least it did for me. Trust me when I tell you, the time you tripped on the stairs in junior high school, showing your day-of-the-week panties to the entire pep rally, will pale in comparison to the moment you, as a white parent, walk into a dance class filled with ten little black girls and their mothers on the day your daughter's hair isn't combed. This embarrassment can scar you for life, or at least for a month. The more your child can blend in, the more comfortable both of you will feel. I can't begin to describe the pride I feel when I meet someone new who asks, "Who did her hair?" and I can honestly say, "I did." The skill of combing my children's hair did not come easily, but it was totally worth it.

## The Technical Information You Need to Read

African-American hair varies from straight to curly. Some children have loose curls, like my daughter Madison. Her loose curls are soft and her hair grows long towards her shoulders. Some children have tight curls, like my daughter McKenzie. Her hair is coarse and grows fuller rather than longer. Other children fall somewhere in the middle. You may hear terms like "good hair" and "bad hair" but don't be fooled — it's all just hair.

Our children's hair is dry and this has to do with the amount of oil produced by the scalp. When you look at books or websites, there are lots of technical terms and confusing jargon about the composition and qualities of hair, so let me offer my real-world explanation. My scalp produces oil to nourish and protect my hair. The oil can easily reach the end of each strand since it is a straight shot. My children's hair is curly and the oil produced by the scalp has too many twists and turns to make it to the end of the strand where it is still needed, making it necessary to add oil to keep the scalp and the hair healthy. It isn't enough just to style a child's hair; the scalp must be treated as well. Every morning, I add oil to my children's hair by applying the oil directly to the scalp. Occasionally, they come to me with itchy spots to which I apply more oil.

> *Picture It* — *You're in the grocery store with your kiddo in the cart when you notice a big dry flaky patch on her scalp. You know it has to itch and it looks terrible. A black mother would run her hand along her own head to gather some oil to put on her child's head. A white mother doesn't have oily hair. What do you do? I carry a small jar of oil in my purse for just this occasion. Hand lotion will work in a pinch. Be prepared — it's a jungle out there!*

## Top 11 Critical Tools Needed to Style a Child's Hair

This list, created by Nicole Hewitt, MSW, for the Pennsylvania Child Welfare Training Program, will get you started putting together the essentials for your child's hair-care kit. [1]

1.  **Combs**

    - Rattail comb (great for making straight parts and removing debris from the hair).
    - Pick (wide teeth allow for combing through thick hair).
    - Wide-tooth comb (helps detangle thick hair during a comb out).

2.  **Brush**

    - You need a soft or medium boar-bristle brush. Avoid brushes with plastic or nylon bristles on them, as they contribute to breakage in the hair.
    - A brush helps to smooth the hair.

3.  **Oil**

    - Good for shine and provides some nutrients. Use oils that contain sage, olive, rosemary, and almond or lavender, which are great for the hair and scalp.
    - Light oils in liquid form (not gel) are best.

4.  **Spray Bottle or Detangler Spray**

    - If using a spray bottle, fill it with one part oil and six parts water.

5.  **Blow Dryer (preferably with a comb attachment)**

    - Aids in quick drying and detangling.

6.  **Hair Ornaments**

    - Bows, ribbons, barrettes, cloth-covered rubber bands (these won't break the child's hair), beads, and knockers (or ponytail holders).

7.  **Hair Pins**

    - To assist in holding some styles securely.

8.  **Hair Clips**

    - To keep hair divided into sections when attempting to style.

9.  **Gel**

    - Helps in styling and luster.

10. **Child's favorite videotape or DVD**

    - Can be an aid in getting children to sit still during a styling process.

11. **Patience**

    - Do not become frustrated with the process. Have fun!

## Lotions, Oils and Hairdressings

There are hundreds of types of oil and most are sold in plastic jars. You can also find oil in a spray bottle, which is great for braids. I really like the brand Carol's Daughter that comes in a pump-spray bottle. I have only found Carol's Daughter on the Sephora website and the website for Carol's Daughter, but your stylist may carry it in the shop. The ingredients are all natural.

When the company first started, the products were mixed in the founder's kitchen sink. Now, Jada Pinkett-Smith and Mary J. Blige are the spokespeople! Since caring for your child's hair takes practice, try different kinds of oils to find the one you like the best. I have found oil to be reasonably priced, so don't be afraid to experiment. If you came to my house right now, you would find a dozen half-used jars of oil under the bathroom sink.

Lanolin and petroleum-based oils will clog the pores and attract lint. For many years I used petroleum-based products because they are the most readily available in almost every store. I recently read about the benefits of natural products made with oils like olive, rosemary, and sage, so we are giving them a try. So far, I love it! My biggest complaint with the petroleum-based products was how much lint ended up on the hair. I was constantly picking rug residue and carpet fuzz out of ponytails! My girls enjoy the process of applying oil because it feels like a scalp massage and who doesn't love that? Use a boar-bristle brush to distribute the oil to the ends of the hair. This type of brush will pick up any lint or fuzzies that may appear in the hair from your kids rolling on the carpet.

A warning: oil can stain clothes and furniture, so be sure to apply it directly to the scalp and allow time for absorption. No one likes re-creating the scene from *Coming to America* when Eric LaSalle's Soul Glow hair grease leaves stains on the sofa.

In addition to oiling the scalp, I also use a dressing, or moisturizer, on the hair. At the moment, I am using a product called Liv that was recommended to me by the person who braids McKenzie's hair. It is a thick white cream that smells wonderful and adds great moisture to the hair. I have used dozens of moisturizing products over the years. Find what works best for you. Adding moisture to the length of the hair goes a long way in creating a beautiful style or hairdo for your child.

There are plenty of products to choose from and your trusted stylist is a great resource. I have used a variety of products, from salon brands like Aveda, Dudley's and my new favorite, Design Essentials, to the Just For Me and Olive Oil brands from the grocery store. They each have pros and cons and once you are familiar with the process, you can make an educated choice.

> *We currently use Aveda products on our 21 month old and have since she was a year old. She has a very tight curl afro that we shampoo and condition once to twice a week. We use several products including Aveda Scalp Benefits conditioner, Brilliant Conditioner, Brilliant Damage Control spray (with chamomile), and Brilliant Universal Styling Crème (with jojoba). We will continue to experiment with other Aveda products as Allie's hair grows and changes. The Aveda staff is always helpful, the company cares for the environment and the products are made from many natural ingredients. Aveda is a [brand] I use and trust on my own hair, so I just cut to the chase for my beautiful daughter and I'm giving her hair (and scalp) a good "head start."*
> — *Leah Ann O'Shieles, mother of two, one of whom is black*

## Where to Find Products and Accessories

The internet and the yellow pages are your best tools in locating the businesses in your community that sell these products. General beauty supply stores like Sally's are a great place to start. You can also find products in salons. My personal favorite places to shop are the black hair-care stores. I visit Kim's Imports on a regular basis in my hometown of Austin to pick up shampoo, oil, and hair accessories. The store resembles a flea market with selections stretching from wall to wall. I have always found the price and the selection to be worth the trip. I don't recommend taking the kids with you; these stores offer one potential child disaster after another, thanks to the amount of stuff in the aisles.

You can even find the products you need in big-box stores like Target. But if your local grocery store and/or Target store do not carry *any* black hair care products, this should be a warning to you about where you live!

## Getting Started: Washing Hair

All of the hair must be washed from the ends to the scalp and rinsed thoroughly. You will find it takes a lot of water to wet the hair. Older kids wash their hair in the shower. With younger kids, it helps to use a handheld sprayer in the bathtub. For a child with tightly curled hair, do not gather the hair on the top of the head, as this will cause more tangles. Make sure you rinse thoroughly after washing, since residue will further dry the hair. Don't wash hair in a circular motion as this will increase the number of tangles. For thicker hair, you may have to wash a couple of times. It is a great idea to use a clarifying shampoo once a month to remove the buildup of oil and other products.

After washing the hair thoroughly, use conditioner to soften the hair. You can use a leave-in conditioner or one that you wash out in the bathtub. If your child's hair is damaged, try a hot-oil or penetrating conditioner. You can use this type of conditioner once a month rather than on weekly basis. The penetrating conditioner is left on the hair for 15 minutes or so with a towel wrapped around the child's head. We find it fun to paint fingernails during this time.

Once you have washed and conditioned it, twist the hair to remove excess water and then wrap it in a clean towel to twist again. Don't rub the hair in a towel the way you might do with your own hair as this also increases the tangles. You'll thank me later!

When I was a child, it wasn't unusual to go to bed with wet hair or to race out the door for school with a still-damp ponytail. Unfortunately, neither of these options is possible for my children. Washing the hair is the beginning of a process that must be completed. Do not let children go to bed with wet hair. The tangles will be horrible and the scalp will be like the Sahara desert. Your child will cry and you will too. Caring for your child's hair is a true commitment of time and I have not found many shortcuts in seven years.

Because your child's hair is naturally dry, you won't need to wash it as often as you would your own. I have found once a week to be the best frequency for my children; however athletics, swimming, and summertime activities may mean more frequent washing, which will require additional moisturizing.

## Hair Combing 101

Little white kids brush their hair, but little black kids comb theirs because of the curls.

After washing my kid's hair and squeezing out excess water in an absorbent towel, I divide the hair into sections using a rattail comb. I use long clips to hold the sections in place, which allows me to work on one section at a time. I start at the ends and work my way to the scalp with a wide-tooth comb. For long hair, I use a hair dryer on each section with an attachment that combs the hair at the same time. You can pick one up at your local Sally's Beauty Supply. For short hair, I avoid the hair dryer because it further dries out the hair. Short hair can be left to air-dry naturally.

Once the hair is dry, I part it in even sections with the rattail comb to apply oil directly to the scalp. It took me a while to accept the oily appearance of my girls' hair because this is a look I avoid on my own head. Trust me when I say you want your daughter's hair and head to appear oily. If it looks full and flat (by flat I mean lacking in oil) like your own, you haven't done it right.

## Five Tips to Comb the Hair of a Small Child

I used to find combing the hair of my youngest kiddos was like wrestling with a greased pig. These tips will help ease the process.

- Put the child in a high chair with a snack, like Cheerios.
- Put the child between your crisscrossed legs on the floor with *Baby Einstein* or a similar video playing in front of you.
- Let her hold the bag of clips, bows, and rubber bands to hand to you as your helper.
- Have someone else hold your child in their lap while reading a book or watching a video — anything distracting.
- Place a child-size chair between your legs in front of a coffee table while you sit on a sofa or chair. Let the child draw while you comb. A movie is helpful too.

## Basic Styling Techniques

Traditionally, we keep little girls' hair in multiple ponytails as a means to gain access to the scalp and keep hair manageable. It is common to use clips, knockers (two balls connected by a rubber band), and other hair accessories. I remember picking up Madison from day care when she was about six months old and her hair was in three ponytails. I laughed out loud at these tiny little ponytails on top of her head, created by the loving hands of her teacher, who explained to me how important it is to get little girls used to this process.

Section the hair into the desired number of ponytails. Make sure the scalp is well oiled and the hair in your hand is not completely dry. You may need to add some lotion, or dressing, to the length of the hair if the hair is dry. I recommend using plastic wraps instead of actual rubber bands since these are easier to take down.

Once the scalp is oiled and the hair is moisturized, it can be parted into sections and then made into ponytails that can be styled in these three ways:

**1. Puffs** are frequently seen on girls. They are literally puffs of hair created by making a ponytail, then picking out the curls, leaving the hair puffy and free.

**2. Basic braids** are created by layering three strands of hair in a certain order. You can braid hair that is already gathered in a ponytail or just pick up a section of hair from the scalp, divide it into three and start braiding.

**3. Basic twists** are created when you separate the hair in the ponytails into two sections and twist. Another popular style is to twist small (one-inch) sections of hair all over the head.

These are perfectly appropriate styles for little girls, though there are millions more you can try. Pay attention to how other black children in your community have their hair done and use these styles as your starting point, because people favor different styles in different parts of the country. In some communities, the small natural afro with a couple of barrettes or a cute headband is common on girls through early elementary school. In other places, that style is used only for young children whose hair is still short. The point is you want your child to look good and fit in. They will get enough attention for having white parents; you don't want them getting more attention because they have white parents who gave them a hairstyle that no black mother in your town would ever do! Hair care will take practice, so don't get upset with yourself if you don't get it right the first time. Combing hair isn't easy and it certainly isn't quick. Your daughter will probably fight you at different times because she doesn't want to sit still or have you in her space. Keep reminding yourself this has to be done for the greater good and how beautiful she will look. You are preparing her for a lifetime of hair care.

## More Advanced Styling Techniques

As your kids grow and their hair gets longer, you can begin to try these more advanced styling techniques.

# Braids

I love braids! They are the answer to every parent's hair prayer! I was surprised to learn that not all African-Americans know how to braid hair. When you find someone who is creative and able to work with your child, you will keep them on your speed dial forever. In the beginning, I had Madison's hair braided only when we went on vacation. This allowed me to leave most of the hair paraphernalia at home rather than in my suitcase. Now I have her hair braided on other occasions as well. Braids can last anywhere from two to five weeks, depending on how you care for the style. Wrapping your child's head in a silk scarf before bedtime helps a lot, along with daily applications of oil.

Cornrows are the most common style of braid. This braid is created by layering three sections of hair, starting at the scalp. The sections of hair cross over top of each other, making the braid sit on top of the head. Cornrows are seen around the world and, in my opinion, rarely look good on white tourists with the exception of Bo Derek. Cornrows can be decorated with barrettes, knockers, and beads or left plain. You can purchase every imaginable color and style of beads at the ethnic hair stores I mentioned earlier. Madison used to insist on pink beads only. For the first day of kindergarten, she chose tiny tiaras to decorate her lovely locks! She loves the sound the beads make as they click together and it is impossible for her to sneak up on anyone. She feels beautiful in braids.

Having my children's hair braided means less stressful mornings and more time to do other things. The braids also protect the hair because it is held close to the head, which makes it a wonderful style for children who have damaged hair when they join your family. You can even wash hair that is braided. The braid is the perfect style.

To find someone who braids hair, check with local black salons, ask African-American teenage girls and women who have great braids, or call a member of the support network you have established. I have found word of mouth to be the best means of finding a skilled braider.

Synthetic hair is often added to braids to create a different look. You can buy hair of every shade and texture to add length and volume to a style. My daughter McKenzie has very short hair that is difficult to grow. I have her hair braided with extensions, or synthetic hair, to give her a real style. She looks like a million bucks and it shows. I am in awe watching McKenzie's hair transform from short and puffy to long and braided. Someday I may have to find some extra hair for me!

## Locks and Twists

Locks and twists are commonly used in both children and adults. Locks are dreadlocks while twists are created by tightly twisting small strands of hair. Twists are made by dividing hair into very small sections but not putting elastic close to the scalp. Each section is divided into two strands and the strands are tightly twisted around each other. The curls in your daughter's hair will link around each other to hold the twist without elastics, though some form of hairdressing is usually applied to the ends for a little extra holding power. Twists stay in for a week or two and can be accessorized with headbands, barrettes, and if long enough, pulled up into ponytails.

If you never took the twists out, they would turn into dreadlocks. Before you put on the Bob Marley CD and have a Rasta moment, consider dreadlocks carefully. Be sure they are an appropriate style for someone your child's age in your community. Dreadlocks are not easily removed like braids and twists.

> *Our family loves beeswax to use at the end*
> *of our daughter's twists. It is a non-petroleum*
> *product and it works wonders.*
> *— Pamela Jarvis, mother of Evie, age 4*

Once the style is in, take care of it with daily oiling and a silk scarf around your child's head at night to maintain the style. While it may come off during the night, the scarf is great in protecting the hair from breakage and keeping ponytails, braids, and twists in place. If your child is adamant about pulling that scarf off, try using a silk pillowcase. My girls changed their tune about the scarf when I brought one home in a fabulous shade of hot pink. Somehow that scarf is able to stay in place throughout the night. Imagine that!

## Perms

When I was a teenager, I used to get a perm every few months to add curl and body to my limp hair. It was a disgusting process that took nearly two hours. There was always the risk of being burned and my sinuses were wiped clean from the chemicals for at least a week. I hated getting a perm but loved the results because the curl lasted through many washings, hence the name.

For black hair, getting a perm, or relaxer, means to straighten the hair. Chemicals are used in a similar way with the same risk of burns and affected sinus cavities. It has become increasingly popular in the last decade to forget the chemicals and keep hair natural and unpermed. As I understand it, hair was originally straightened in an effort to make it look like the hair of white women, which was considered culturally acceptable and more desirable. As African-Americans embraced their history and culture, hair trends have changed. It is now popular for black women to have natural, or authentic, hairstyles by maintaining the curls with which they were born, though some women use relaxers to help make super-curly hair more manageable.

Black mothers have shared varying opinions on this subject with me over the years. It is a deeply personal decision whether or not to perm or relax your daughter's hair. Once you relax the hair, maintaining the look means regular, lengthy and expensive visits to the hair salon. If you decide not to perm the hair again, your child must endure a process similar to that of white women growing out their bangs; there will be a period of a month or more when the hair is in transition from relaxed to curly, and sometimes it's not pretty. I chose not to perm my children's hair because I feel they are too young and I am not willing to maintain this somewhat expensive process. Plus, I love their curls!

Some families choose not to perm hair but will occasionally straighten the curls with a ceramic flat iron. This tool creates a completely different look and can be a lot of fun. Of course, flat irons are popular with almost everyone regardless of color. I learned from my own stylist when she first used the flat iron on my hair that it is very hot and it can dry the hair quickly. For these reasons, I don't use the flat iron very often on my daughter's hair, save for dance recitals and Easter celebrations when appearing elegant is extremely important to a little girl.

## Salon Care

Develop a relationship with a stylist who can work with you on a regular basis to maintain your child's hair. I recommend interviewing a stylist to determine how comfortable she is working with kids and how many appointments she books in a single time slot. Remember to ask to see some samples of her work.

*Cultural Moment* — When I make an appointment with my hair-stylist, I am fairly certain I will be in her chair at the designated appointment time. This is not the case in the black salon. You could be there for hours. Make sure to find out how many appointments are booked at the same time and how long you should anticipate being there so you can plan appropriately to keep your child entertained. In preparation for your salon visit, pop in the Queen Latifah movie, Beauty Shop.

I have even booked an appointment with a stylist to help me master a hairstyle that I can do at home. These professionals are a great resource. The trick is finding the one who is right for you.

*Best Practice* — If possible, call ahead to the salon and introduce yourself over the phone. Explain that you are white and your child is not. I have found it easier to walk into an unfamiliar salon when I have developed a relationship over the phone with a stylist. Believe me, this is the place you will stick out the most on your first visit. Not to worry; it will never be as hard as it is the first time!

The best way to find a stylist is through word of mouth. Find someone who has a good reputation for working well with children. Once you find the right person, ask for a consultation so he or she can look at your child's hair and answer any questions about style and upkeep before you make a styling appointment. Most black grandmothers tell me I shouldn't cut my children's hair because it takes too long to grow, but this is another old wives' tale. Hair needs to be trimmed regularly. Dead ends aren't good for me or my girls!

Madison isn't crazy about going to the salon, which means I have to prepare her for the experience in the days leading up to the appointment. McKenzie, on the other hand, jumps right into the chair. The stylist we use lets me hold Madison's hand and occasionally I have her sit in my lap while her hair is styled. Be sure to bring any toys, books, or "lovies" that will put your child at ease during the appointment.

# Boys' Hair

For little boys, the custom in the black community is to wait until his first birthday to cut the hair. I am told cutting the hair before the first birthday alters the development of the hair follicle and affects the hair pattern. Without a doubt, caring for a little boy's hair is much easier than caring for a little girl's hair. However, the scalp must still be oiled and hair, if any, must be combed to keep it manageable.

The styles for boys vary depending on the length of hair and what is popular in your community. "In my son's school," explains Aimee Estep, "boys wear very short to short hair, small and medium afros, cornrows and twists." If your child's hair is long enough to do cornrows or twists, the process and care are the same as for girls' hair. For short haircuts, two things are important: the edge and the shape. Once a little boy starts getting his hair cut, there should be a crisp line at the edge of the hair along his forehead and sides of his face, as well as at the back of his neck. If hair is cut very close to the scalp, upkeep means a weekly washing and daily oiling or lotion applied to the hair and scalp. You then use a flat brush to brush the little bit of hair there is, which a barber explains helps train the hair to lay the way you want it.

If your child has a small afro, the hair should be trimmed regularly so there are no little pieces of hair sticking up above the other hairs and to keep the shape round. Regular upkeep includes the weekly washing and daily oiling and lotion, followed by picking the hair into a neat shape (meaning round — no triangles or trapezoids here!). To keep short hair and small afros looking good, you need to take your son to the barber every two to three weeks.

Now it may be intimidating for some, particularly single women, to make the initial visit to the barbershop because it is such a masculine place, and it brings to mind a lot of worries about raising black boys. You will probably find it not as intimidating as you imagined! Start by choosing a barber you and your son really like. Take the same time and care to find a barber as you would a stylist for your daughter. Ask friends, neighbors, teachers, and other members of your support team for recommendations and then go visit the shop.

## Tips for Sizing Up a Barbershop

When you first go into a barbershop, pay attention to the atmosphere.

- Is the barber in a hurry or is he or she engaging with the child?
- Does the barber explain the tools of the trade and their purpose?
- Is the shop clean?
- Can you hear swear words or other adult-oriented discussion in the shop? If so, find a new barber.
- Do you feel comfortable in the shop? Does your son?

Barbershops are very different places from hair salons. There will be lots of men, lots of banter, probably a TV on. Some men will be getting their hair cut and some will just be visiting with other people. In my experience, your child will be expected to sit in the chair alone — no sitting on Mama's lap! If your child is young or especially wriggly, one barber may gently hold his head still while another clips the hair. Sideburns will be clipped also. If you ask, the barber will give you good advice on hair care and products for your son. For your child's first cut, find out the least busy time and go then. Most shops do not accept appointments, so show up with a book to read with your child or something to do in case you have to wait. This is also a good time to talk to your son about what the barber is doing.

In some neighborhoods, you may find men who cut hair at home and this can be a viable option as well, particularly for children (such as those with special needs) who may find the noise level and activity in a shop disconcerting. If you do not have a barbershop where you live (and again, this is a red flag about your community), find a stylist who cuts black hair. In theory, all stylists are trained to cut different kinds of hair but some do it better than others. Make the effort to help your child look good because it will help him be part of the black community.

## Babies' Hair

Babies are born with varying amounts of hair. As an infant, Madison's hair was silky and wavy, giving me a false sense of hope that I could draw from my own hair experience. The same was true of my youngest daughter, Morgan, whose hair was soft and curly as an infant. However, the curl increases as they grow.

Infants require hair care as well, though on a simpler level. A baby's hair should be washed with a mild shampoo once a week and a small amount of oil should be applied to the scalp. It is perfectly acceptable to keep a baby's hair natural and free. If you decide to put the hair into ponytails, be very careful of the soft spot. Don't use rubber bands or hair accessories because they tend to find their way into the mouth of all babies.

## The Four S's to Guard Against!

As a mother of black children, you'll find that the four S's — sandboxes, swimming pools, sleepovers, and self-styling — are not your friends!

## Sandboxes

When I was growing up, I loved to play in the sandbox. I often see children in a sandbox at a park or playground and think back to the times I spent in sandboxes. Unfortunately, this is an activity I don't share with my children.

> **Picture It** — *The white mother of an African-American daughter attends a parenting class at a local church, leaving her four-year-old daughter, in the care of the nursery staff. When Mom returns to the nursery, she sees her daughter sitting in the sandbox on the playground. The mother spends the next three hours in the bathtub with the daughter trying to get the sand out of her head. The white childcare workers were unaware of the disastrous effects of sand on the hair of African-American children. This became another teaching moment where the parent shared some insights into black culture with childcare providers.*

This is the deal with sandboxes: the tiny grains of sand become trapped in the curls of the hair and work their way to the scalp. The sand can rub sores on the scalp and can cause hair to fall out. If your child gets into a sandbox, remove the sand immediately by brushing, combing, picking, or eventually in the bathtub. It isn't easy and in my experience, both of you will cry, but it is absolutely necessary. As parents we never want our kids to experience pain, and the sand will cause damage like you never thought possible. Beware!

> *Keep out of the sand! I recommend not having a sandbox at your house, minimizing the amount of time kids spend in a sandbox, and having them wear a head covering (scarf or hat) if they do. Sand will scratch the scalp and cut the hair off at the roots if it gets down in there. It has to be completely removed immediately, which isn't easy. When you leave your kids with others, and there is any chance of a sand encounter, let them know this, too.*
>
> *— Pamela Jarvis, mother of Evie, age 4*

## Swimming

In addition to threatening the hairstyle, the chlorine in swimming pools can damage hair. It is important to remember how delicate your child's hair is, so take precautions to protect what you have worked hard to achieve. We have a beautiful collection of swim caps that are used every summer when taking a dip in the pool. The swim cap protects the hair from water, keeping the head completely dry. When your daughter reaches an age where the only way she will wear a swim cap is if she's in the lane next to Michael Phelps, plan on keeping her hair in braids, rinsing the hair after swimming and applying additional moisturizer to the hair.

## Sleepovers

The white mother of a nine-year-old black daughter sends her to a sleepover at a white friend's house. The daughter leaves home with a beautiful head of skinny cornrows and returns the next morning looking like Don King — not a good look on a little girl! The mother of the white friend took down every braid so the girls could shower before bed. She had no idea that braids don't come out every night and that it takes hours to braid an entire head of hair. And she had no idea how black people care for their hair after washing it. Both mothers felt awful.

When your child starts spending the night away from home, be gentle yet clear to non-black parents about hair care. Even when surrounded by people of different races, white people tend to have limited information about the basics of another race. Let them know that your daughter does not need to wash her hair that night, that she has a shower cap to cover her hair in the shower, and that she has lotion she can apply to her hair. If your child is too young to do this on her own, send a cute hat with her and plan to pick her up in the morning with time to style her hair. If you are going to be on a business trip or something that keeps you away from home for more than a night or two, let your child stay with black friends or make specific plans for your child's hair care. Braids and some braid spray or the help of a good friend can be crucial here. The same advice applies to sleep-away camps: give your child a hairstyle she can maintain and be specific to any staff about hair care.

## Self-Styling

You look around the kindergarten classroom and see the children who obviously dress themselves and the crazy ponytails and too many headbands of little girls who style their own hair. Repeat after me: this will not be my child. Now say it again. As your child gets older, she will learn to style her own hair but you will still need to make sure it is done properly for two reasons. The first reason is: tangles will form if the hair is not combed well, creating a larger problem. Second, the appearance of your child's hair has added importance in the black community. Let your child help select the hairstyle (braids, twists or puffs) and the hair accessories, but the parent should do the actual work. Slowly teach the skills of washing and combing as you continue to ensure the finished product looks good.

## Practice, Practice, Practice

Congratulations! You are well on your way to mastering the art of hair care! It isn't easy and you should be proud of yourself! As parents and especially mothers, we tend to be hard on ourselves. Personally, I have a Type A personality that insists on perfection. However, learning this craft takes time and practice. While I am regularly complimented on my children's hair, I still have a lot to learn. My hairstyling skills are still a work in progress. My goal is to share some of the lessons I have learned the hard way. This is the time to be gentle to your spirit. Keep practicing and maintain your commitment to learning a new skill out of love for your kiddo.

## The Ten Commandments of Black Hair Care

1. Thou shalt not wash your child's hair every day.
2. Thou shalt not treat your child's hair as your do your own.

3. Thou shalt apply oil to your child's scalp daily.

4. Thou shalt comb hair on a regular basis despite tears, screams, and tantrums.

5. Thou shalt commit yourself to learning the art of hair maintenance.

6. Thou shalt seek professional help from a licensed stylist when in doubt.

7. Thou shalt practice, practice, practice.

8. Thou shalt avoid sandboxes.

9. Though shalt not take every piece of advice offered to you regarding hair and skin.

10. Though shalt not let younger children style their own hair.

# Chapter 9

## Skin

*If we don't stand up for children, then we don't stand up for much.* — Marian Wright Edelman

Our children come in every shade of black. When Madison and Morgan were newborns, I marveled how the pigment of their skin darkened as the days and weeks passed. I was told to pay attention to the color of Madison's ears because this would be her final shade of brown. I was a new mother when I heard this old wives' tale, but it is one I have found to be spot on most of the time.

My daughter's skin is velvety brown, like dark chocolate, and I love the way it shines when I cover her in lotion. I have learned a lot over the years about what to do and what not to do with her skin. I've made mistakes and borne the shame of having it look terrible when out in public. Maybe you have made the same mistakes too or perhaps you are reading this book when your babies are still small and you are still learning. Hopefully, I can save you the walk of shame most white parents must take at some point when our child of color has ashy skin or wild hair. Believe me when I say everyone is watching, whether you realize it or not. For this very reason, I carry a big tube of their lotion in my purse at all times for those unexpected ashy moments.

My experience in parenting children of color has been that the darker the skin, the drier it will be. I am not a dermatologist, but I first noticed the dryness of the skin when caring for our first foster child. She had beautiful skin, but I realized how dull and gray, or ashy, it would become between diaper changes. I started applying Johnson's Baby Lotion to her legs during every diaper change, but it wasn't enough. The Johnson's lotion seemed like water on her skin even though it moisturized my own skin beautifully.

This is when I discovered not all lotion is made the same. The majority of lotions on the market today contain a high proportion of water. The water content makes it possible to pour a puddle of lotion into your hand. Brands like Suave, Jernigan, Vaseline Intensive Care and Johnson's are perfect for my skin but do very little to moisturize my children's skin. I needed something thicker to meet their skin care needs. Our pediatrician recommended Aquaphor when Morgan developed some eczema on her arm as an infant and I have been in love with it ever since. Aquaphor is the consistency of Vaseline, which is what many African-Americans used to care for their skin as children. I have black friends who tell me they still use Vaseline today, especially during the winter when their dark skin is particularly dry. Granted, Vaseline is less expensive than Aquaphor, which retails for about $10 per container, but I have an aversion to plain Vaseline that I am unable to explain.

All three of my kiddos are slathered in Aquaphor upon exiting the bathtub when their skin is still soft and supple from the water. We apply more lotion every morning when they're getting dressed. You can even use Aquaphor as a lip balm in place of ChapStick! Other great brands that offer beautiful hydration are Lubriderm, Keri, are Eucerin. It may take some time to find the right brand for your child, but the results are worth it. The dull, ashy appearance of the skin immediately disappears with the addition of ample lotion of the brands listed above. You will be blown away by the shiny, healthy look of their skin!

It is common for eczema to develop on the limbs of black babies when their skin becomes too dry. Definitely consult your pediatrician to ensure the patches of dry skin you are seeing are, in fact, eczema. You can treat eczema without prescriptions by applying intense moisturization to the affected areas.

Eczema can develop easily from over-bathing your infant. When I was a baby, it was standard practice for me to get a bath every day. As parents, we typically do for our children what was done for us. That is wonderful advice in most every other area of parenting except this one. Do not bathe your black baby every day. Her skin will become too dry from the repeated exposure to water and soap. Instead, give him a bath every few days, unless, of course, there is an accident that requires immediate attention. And I know you know what I mean. Bathing your baby every few days does not mean your child is dirty. This is the best practice, in my experience, in caring for her skin. Use a mild soap like Lever 2000 or Dove when you bathe your child. Moisturize his entire body immediately after drying off from the tub to achieve the best results.

As your child grows older, the frequency of baths can increase. I have chosen to bathe my children every other day given their level of activity. I often speak with parents who have their children bathe daily, but more often than not their children are older and nearing puberty. For my seven and four year olds, every other day is perfect. And never forget — moisturize, moisturize, moisturize! Not only will your child's skin look better but they will have less discomfort from scratchy dryness.

At some point during your baby's childhood, she is going to fall down and get hurt. Or he will jump out of a tree or fall off a bike, making a cut in the skin. Unlike your own skin, our children's skin scars very easily. For this reason, I keep a jar of cocoa butter cream on hand to apply to scrapes or cuts. Do not apply it to open wounds! Once the wound has closed, begin applying the cocoa butter as often as possible. This will help the healing process and usually reduce the appearance of a scar. The cocoa butter even helps when your infant or toddler scratches their face with fingernails.

# Chapter 10

## Culture

*The decision to have a child is to accept that your heart will forever walk outside of your body.* — Katherine Hadley

Writing this book has been a labor of love. I have worked on it for two years and, in the process, have conducted a series of focus groups to glean the experience, strength, and hope of other transracial families. During the course of the focus group on culture, a mother asked me to define African-American culture. Wow, that is a big one! I can give examples of culture, I can recognize cultural opportunities, but to define culture is a tall order.

There are countless volumes of books sitting on shelves in countless libraries and bookstores on the topic of African-American culture. There is no way I can begin to cover thousands of years of history in just a dozen pages. However, I *can* give other white parents the Cliff Notes version, by showing you how your family can get involved in the cultural opportunities that are available in many communities. I strongly recommend finding the occasions that suit your family and remaining open to learning as much as you can about the heritage of your child. Visit the local library or bookstore to flip through some of the thousands of books that exist on the subject of African-American culture. For now, I will share with you the lessons I have learned over the years.

African-American culture is obviously rooted in Africa. According to Wikipedia, "it is a blend of ...sub-Saharan and Sahelean cultures. Although slavery greatly restricted the ability of Americans of African descent to practice their cultural traditions, many practices, values, and beliefs survived and ... blended with European-American culture.... The result is a unique and dynamic culture."

As I began the research for this chapter, I turned to my number one networking resource and online community of support, Facebook, to begin a dialogue with friends about ways to define African-American culture. What I discovered is that the culture is fluid and at the same time, rich in tradition. Granted, this makes raising a child of another culture a bit tricky, but there is a freedom in this fluidity as well. In "Black Unlike Me," a *New York Times* magazine article by Jana Wolff (February, 1999), the author describes the experience of raising a member of another race. "It must be very hard," she reflects, "for a child to have, as tour guides, parents who are tourists themselves. The risk is that the culture being visited will be reduced to its souvenirs."

Good news, my friends: there is wiggle room for the well-intentioned adoptive parents of black youth in America. In my focus group meetings, I asked some black friends, "What does African-American culture mean to you?" Here is what they had to say.

Michelle Freeman, seminary student and community activist:

"I will use the term 'black' because, I too, do not identify with African-American (probably because of my age). I believe black culture is so rich and varied that it defies explaining or defining it in any short order. Our culture embodies our music, our spirituality, our worship, our faith, our beliefs, our morals, values, commonalities, our grooming and so many other aspects of our lives. Most blacks identify with Liberation Theology which speaks to the willingness of our culture to find truth and justice in our desire to live life on life's terms by identifying the struggle of our ancestors to gain civil rights and equality in society. Our ancestors painted a rich tapestry for our generation and generations to come. We do try to cling to our African descent but truth is, our culture is shaped by our experiences here in America and while we can look to our [predecessors] in Africa for inspiration, much of our existence is shaped by our culture right here in the States. There are no rules, morals or values written in stone in the black community and we are constantly evolving."

Jerome Brown, newsman, father of 2:

"What does African-American culture mean to me? It's everything! I graduated from a historically black college (Jackson State University), I joined a historically black fraternity (Kappa), and I attend a predominantly black church. My wife is black [and] is the mother of my black children.

My social life centers on this culture. Those were/are my choices.

"My parents took us to the black events to create pride and the understanding of my heritage and lineage but they taught me to accept all cultures, so I went to everything they could expose us too. Your challenge is to raise those kids with love and to tell them who they are and to accept all cultures. One day they will have choices to make too and my prayer is that you have done all you can to prepare them for such choices."

Kevin Hofmann, author of *Growing Up Black in White*, father of 2:

"I found out, growing up, culture included food, family, music, and beliefs. One of the things I grieved was the loss of culture that I didn't have because I was raised by a white family. It wasn't my parents' fault because they couldn't teach me what they didn't know. I grieved the loss of things like music. My black friends had an intimate knowledge of black music that I just didn't have, since they grew up with it. The belief part was a huge part too. It included beliefs about white privilege, inequality and an unequal system we were a part of."

Davra Harris, mother:

"I also have found that within the African-American culture, it can vary from family to family! I really think that the true essence of our culture is based upon our history! There are so many things that African-Americans do today that were born from our ancestors, for example, jumping the broom [at weddings]. We eat certain parts of a pig today because that is what was fed to our ancestors. I have an uncle who is Muslim. As we all know, Muslims do not eat pork at all. I couldn't understand why. But now I understand...some parts of our history [example, pork eating] feel as though it is a sign of oppression. The African-American culture, to me, is a big melting pot of *color* and *love*!"

Georgia Chambers, seminary student and community activist:

"Black culture is a creative culture. As a matter of fact it was created throughout time according to what our ancestors had available to them. This includes many facets such as the clothing, food, religion, music, knowledge, self-care, etc. Black people really don't have a true inherited culture. We try to mimic African heritage and we have stereotypical foods that we eat, but black culture (especially nowadays) varies individually. There really is not a 'written in stone' definition of black culture."

As transracial families, we must recognize the importance of exposing our children to cultural opportunities as often as possible. Our babies are only in our care for a brief period in the grand scheme of their lifetime and they must know how to live in this world as a person of color. How do we teach them? We show them what it looks like to live as a black person in America since we cannot model that example ourselves. As my friends assured me, there is no set-in-stone definition for African-American culture. There are, however, central themes that are consistent in most conversations and studies of culture.

## Music

While I cannot verify this statement, I think it is safe to assume Adam and Eve probably enjoyed music. Music is everywhere and has been since the beginning of time. The African tradition of drumming still influences the music we hear on the radio today. From the drumming and singing in Africa to the gospel music of the slaves, black culture values music. Think of all the forms of music that have been shaped or influenced by the black experience — jazz, blues, rock and roll, R&B, country, rap, and the list goes on. Music is big.

I loved the sitcom *Designing Women* and often quote the great Julia Sugarbaker, brilliantly portrayed by the late Dixie Carter. In one episode, Julia decides to have her house included in the tour of homes by the Atlanta Historical Society. The people from the historical society make Julia jump through hoops of fire to be part of their elitist tour of white privilege. Having reached the end of her rope and her patience, Julia announces that her home is no longer qualified to be part of the tour because her grandfather once listened to a Nat King Cole album. Julia goes on to kick everyone out of her house and removes her home from the tour.

That episode always made me laugh because the idea that music is black or white is such an archaic notion. Music is music. Music is timeless and free of color. We move to and mimic the sounds that make us feel good, inspired, and energized. Music touches a place deep within each us, making a personal connection with the soul. Music has influenced black culture in ways too many to count.

How can we expose our children to their culture through music?

Keep music in your home. Expose your children to all kinds of music, allowing it to become part of your daily routine. My daughters begin shouting song requests the minute we enter the minivan, and we're in that minivan a lot! Right now their number one most requested artist is Justin Bieber, who is the pop flavor of the year. Justin Bieber is a white, 13-year-old cutie pie and a protégé of the R&B singer, Usher. Artists like Ludacris have collaborated with Justin on this CD and the influence of black culture is apparent. I try to balance the Taylor Swift and Justin Bieber music with the Cheetah Girls, Raven-Symoné, and Alicia Keys. Find the musical taste of your kiddos by exposing them to a variety of musical styles and sounds.

Madison and McKenzie have been heavily influenced by the gospel music heard at their preschool, Mt. Sinai Christian Academy. They are both passionate about music and I love to see them singing with their eyes closed and arms waving. McKenzie, in particular, loves to listen to Bible songs when we are alone in the minivan. She knows every word to "Swing Low Sweet Chariot." I am incredibly thankful to Mrs. Joyce Daniel at Mt. Sinai Christian Academy for her love of gospel music that she shares so freely with my children. I love attending performances at the preschool to see the children sing from the heart the traditional songs taught to them by Mrs. Daniel. She is an amazing lady and we are blessed to have her spiritual and musical influence in our home.

One of Madison's friends recently began taking African drumming lessons in combination with a dance class. I can hardly wait to enroll Madison because she loves to dance. I think this is an incredible opportunity for children of color in this part of the world to connect with their heritage.

What opportunities exist in your area? Check the internet or even the phone book for music lessons offered in the traditionally black areas of your town or city. Look for drumming classes or African dance. Sign up to receive emails for events taking place in the black community. In Austin, we have a wonderful store called Mitchie's Gallery that sells art and books. Mitchie's plays host to a multitude of community and cultural events including children's story time, children's arts and crafts, book signings, poetry readings, and so much more. This store is a giant resource for families like mine and I look forward to the weekly emails about upcoming events and cultural opportunities in the city. Stay connected to your child's cultural community and look for the opportunities to expose your little ones to music.

## Religion

I remember growing up in Mississippi where church was a weekly tradition that could not be missed unless you were actively vomiting or had a fever. On those rare occasions that I did not attend service at my predominantly white Methodist church, I would stay home to watch the televised service of my friend April's church. Wow! These people knew how to worship! I loved the hats, the music, the sermon, the passion of the whole experience. And I wished I could attend.

I once asked April if white people were welcome at her church. I don't remember exactly what she said, but I know the message I received was yes, white people are welcome, but we don't put them on television. I never had a chance to attend a service at April's church, but I think I may go home to Hattiesburg in November if her dad, Johnny DuPree, becomes the governor of Mississippi. That sounds like the perfect reason to worship together.

To understand why religion is so important to African-American culture, you must take into consideration the centuries of oppression imposed on this group of people. Stripped of all dignity, the slaves held tightly to faith. During the first century of slavery, their African religions first blended with Christianity and eventually were supplanted by Christian beliefs and traditions. In the church and in Jesus they found love, acceptance, and freedom. The cultural significance of religion is enormous. Jennifer Danvers of Taylor, Texas, recognizes the importance of a church community to children. Jennifer was raised in the Jewish faith and considers herself to be Jewish today. However, she attends a Christian church for the sake of her black sons.

You will also find a large number of people of color identifying as Muslim. The Islamic faith was born in the Middle East in the sixth century A.D. and spread first to north Africa and then south over much of the African continent. Following the end of slavery and during the

Depression, the African-American community began to incorporate traditional African practices into their daily routines as cultural pride and heritage began to grow. More and more people of color became Muslim during this period and the faith gained nationwide recognition when two very famous public figures — Muhammad Ali and Malcolm X — converted to Islam. While there are larger numbers of Christians within the black community, be prepared to meet many Muslims as you navigate the culture of your children.

To incorporate religion into your home, ask for recommendations of predominantly black churches or, at the very least, racially diverse churches in your area. Black friends or members of your support group are great resources for this information. Try checking the phone book or the internet. If you don't know someone who attends the church you're interested in and who would be willing to accompany you during the first visit, try contacting the church directly. I find it easier to have potentially awkward conversations over the phone rather than in person. Introduce yourself to the pastor or other staff member and explain the dynamics of your family. Kindly ask for their support and assistance in your effort to incorporate religion as a cultural experience into your family. I have always received a warm reception from the black community when I have humbly and respectfully asked for help in doing the right thing for my children. This won't be an easy conversation for many people, but I hope you can see the necessity. Again, how far are you willing to stretch your neck out for your babies?

## Food

I love food. There are very few cultural cuisines I do not enjoy and African-American food has got to be my favorite! Of course, I grew up in Mississippi so I know good food.

In my experience, adoptive parents tend to be Type A personalities who make a conscious effort to eat healthy foods. In order to connect with your child's culture through food, you need to put aside everything you know about nutrition and give in to the power of comfort food. Think fried chicken, macaroni and cheese, cornbread, green beans heavily seasoned with bacon, and grits.

Traditionally called "soul food," the cultural cuisine of the black community is a labor of love, rich in flavor and tradition. I am told the menu is testament to the creativity of black mothers who had to make something out of nothing and make it taste good. Like so many other cultures, the experience of the food is not just about the consumption but also about the cooking.

A favorite soul-food restaurant in Austin recently closed when the owner and chief cook decided to retire. Dot Hewitt is in her 70s and, without a doubt, deserves to retire. She and her late husband operated Dot's Place for 30 years in Austin, serving down-home traditional meals to the masses. Her restaurant burned to the ground several years ago and having no insurance, she turned to the community for help. It seemed like every Austin radio station was involved in calling for help to rebuild Dot's Place because people came out by the boatload to donate money for Dot to reopen her amazing eatery. Dot's Place was what that other southern favorite, Luby's Cafeteria, would have been had a black woman run the kitchen. The entire building used to be filled with good smells that are born from a lot of love and a frying pan.

To incorporate the food of your child's culture, consider introducing foods to the family such as collard greens, homemade biscuits, and macaroni and cheese made from scratch. Spend time together in the kitchen as a family preparing meals. Challenge yourself to perfect a dish your family enjoys, something you prepare from start to finish in your own kitchen. To get ideas for what to prepare in your home, visit a restaurant that features soul food.

I am so thankful to have had the opportunity to eat at Dot's Place so many times over the years and I am looking for the next best place in Austin to get my fix of down-home cooking. Check the internet or the phone book to find the restaurants in your area. Don't expect valet parking or any pretense, because soul food is about filling your belly inexpensively and filling your heart at the same time. In my experience, soul food is real, unpretentious, and true to the roots of black culture. If you're in an area with little cultural influence, turn to movies like *Soul Food* for ideas.

## Art

Art is another great tradition within the African-American culture. And don't just think paintings because there are so many different media for artistic expression within the culture. I love to look at handwoven baskets, oil paintings, photographs, and much more.

A few years ago, my family attended the annual Pecan Street Festival, held twice a year in downtown Austin. We discovered an amazing artist who painted the most vivid pictures of black children. We fell in love with her work and bought a piece right on the street, as we munched on a turkey leg from a few stalls back. Her name is Tonya Engel and she now lives in Brooklyn, N.Y. I am so thankful to have found her years ago and I hope to continue adding pieces by her to our collection.

Jennifer Danvers of Taylor, Texas, and mother of three is an avid art buyer/collector. I was tickled by the stories she tells of the staff of many art galleries in Austin knowing her daughter's first name because they visited the gallery so often. Jennifer went on to share with me two of her favorite artists, Janel Jefferson and Suzanne Berry. Hanging beautiful pieces of art that reflect the likeness of your child is a wonderful way to incorporate culture into your home. Learn as much as you can about the artist and the story behind the piece of work so your art collection can be more than just a souvenir of another culture.

## Literature

I have been a lover of literature for most of my life and the authors who have made the greatest impression on me have been the greats like Maya Angelou and Toni Morrison. I had the opportunity to see Dr. Maya Angelou speak to a captivated audience in Austin almost five years ago. I said to Kim as I walked to the car, "I can die now. She is amazing." Thankfully, I did not die and my life is all the richer for having been in her presence if only for just an hour.

I was introduced to Toni Morrison in high school by the greatest English teacher who ever walked the Earth, in my humble opinion. Lois Rodgers assigned the class the joy of reading *The Bluest Eye* and later I found other treasures by Toni Morrison.

These two writers in particular have a way with words I can only dream of someday having. Their descriptive abilities are awe inspiring, giving a fly-on-the-wall insight into black culture.

Do you have any books on your shelf with brown faces on the back? More than likely you have some children's books with brown faces, but do you have any books for adults with positive portrayals of African-Americans? Do you receive magazines in your mailbox with people of color on the cover? Do you value the information provided by *Jet* magazine or *Essence*? Do your children have the chance to see you acquiring a Ph.D. in transracial adoption? Let them. Your kiddos are worth it.

## Traditions

African-American culture has countless traditions passed down from one generation to the next. Unfortunately, no one passed those traditions on to white adoptive parents like us, so we must learn them for ourselves. Here are some of my favorite traditions from black culture.

My favorite tradition has to be the jumping of the broom. In the days of slavery, couples were not allowed to marry in the traditional ways white couples married. There was no legal ceremony or benefit. The tradition of jumping the broom was born from necessity. Slaves designed their own marriage ceremonies, which ended with the bride and groom jumping over a broom, one of the few tools available to them to use as a prop. I am always tickled when I see black celebrities incorporating this cultural tradition into their modern-day wedding ceremony. The tradition continues. I hope my daughters will choose to jump the broom when the time rolls around, which I also hope is many, many years down the road.

Another tradition we enjoy is the celebration of Juneteenth. This day commemorates the emancipation of slaves in Texas. Although Abraham Lincoln signed the Emancipation Proclamation on September 22, 1862, the slaves in Texas did not receive word until June 19, 1865. Informal celebrations of Juneteenth have been going on in Texas for more than a century and Texas became the first state to formally recognize and celebrate the holiday. Juneteenth is now spreading around the country. As of March 2010, 35 states recognize Juneteenth as a state holiday or state holiday observance. Those states include Alaska, Arkansas, California, Colorado, Connecticut, Delaware, Florida, Idaho, Indiana, Illinois, Iowa, Kansas, Kentucky, Louisiana, Massachusetts, Michigan, Minnesota, Missouri, Nebraska, New Jersey, New Mexico, New York, North Carolina, Ohio, Oklahoma, Oregon, South Carolina, Tennessee, Texas, Vermont, Virginia, Washington, West Virginia, Wisconsin, and Wyoming. The day is celebrated in my hometown of Austin with a parade between the University of Texas and the traditionally black Huston-Tillotson

College, followed by a community festival. Look for Juneteenth celebrations in your own state. This is a great way to get involved with the African-American community.

Kwanzaa is a celebration around Christmastime that celebrates African heritage and culture. Similar to the Jewish celebration of Hanukkah, a candle is lit every day for seven days in the celebration of Kwanzaa. The holiday was created by Maulana Karenga in 1966 to "give blacks an alternative to the existing holiday and give blacks an opportunity to celebrate themselves and history, rather than simply imitate the practice of the dominant society." As time has passed, the celebration of Kwanzaa has become more inclusive of Christians and serves as a celebration of family, community, and culture.

I have purchased several children's books over the years to read to my daughters about the practice of Kwanzaa. I admit I have not fully incorporated this tradition into our home, but I can say I have grown more aware and more knowledgeable of the season as the years have passed. I have also learned that not every person of color celebrates Kwanzaa, as it is a personal commitment to do so. I often tell parents not to feel obligated to include Kwanzaa celebrations into their homes but definitely to remain open to learning more about this holiday.

As many grains of sand as there are on the beach, there are traditions in the heritage of your child and contributions by members of their racial community to the world at large. Fortunately, you have the opportunity to pick and choose which ones are meaningful for your family. The goal is to continually expose your child to her heritage in an effort to build in her a positive racial identity. As transracial adoptive parents, we do not have the luxury of sitting on our laurels in hopes our children will be just fine with only our love and adoration. We must be proactive, diligently providing models to show our babies how to be the people God created them to be.

# Chapter 11

## Final Thoughts

I was sitting in the lobby of the dance school waiting for Madison's class to finish when the studio door opened and the beautiful little dancers poured out. Maddie's teacher asked me to step inside to speak with me privately and I cringed. She closed the door behind me and explained that the authenticity of Maddie's family was called into question during the class.

"What exactly does that mean?" I asked her.

"We were talking about families while the girls were changing from ballet to tap shoes," she explained. "Jessica told Maddie that her family is weird because her moms are white. She went on to question how Maddie's family could even be a real one since she doesn't have a dad and everyone is a different color. Maddie just folded and became very upset. I wanted you to know that I interceded and talked about how many different kinds of families there are, but I knew you would want to know what happened."

I hate finding out that I need to drag someone else's kid behind the building to knock some sense into them! I walked out of the studio blinking back tears and praying I wouldn't cross paths with Jessica or her mother. I was mad. How dare you hurt my baby's feelings! I tried to talk to Madison in the car on the way home about what happened during class, but she wasn't talking.

I stewed about the morning's events for the rest of the day. I even cried. Behind the anger was hurt. I would move heaven and earth for any of my children and I needed to figure out a way to handle the situation. I prayed about the issue all week long and by the time we left for dance class the following Saturday, I had a solid plan prepared.

As it turned out, Jessica and her mother parked next to us and both families were exiting our cars at the same time. We exchanged the usual morning pleasantries and then I said to Jessica's mother, "Hey, I wanted to check with you about some questions I think Jessica has about our family. I understand there was a conversation about different kinds of families during class last week and I wanted to make sure Jessica has all the facts. I thought it might be helpful if I answered any of her questions directly." My tone of voice remained upbeat and genuine.

Jessica, who is a little older than Madison, looked at her mother and nodded. Her mother looked confused but asked Jessica if she wanted to talk to me alone or would she like her to stay. Surprisingly, Jessica said she wanted to talk to me alone and to my shock, her mother said okay. Keep in mind I had earned this mother's trust and respect by sitting with her every Saturday morning for the last two years while our daughters danced in the next room.

Jessica and I stood beneath a tree in the parking lot. Madison was close enough to me to become one with my thigh. Jessica's mother walked a few feet away to give us some privacy. I asked Jessica if she had any questions she wanted to ask me directly. I promised her I would tell the truth and clear up any confusion.

"How is Madison black and you aren't?" the six-year-old asked.

"You know how you used to live in your mommy's tummy and then you were born?" I asked. "Well, Madison lived in someone else's tummy before she came to live with me when she was born. The lady whose tummy Maddie lived in is black and that makes Maddie black, just like you and your mom are black. We call that lady Maddie's birth mom because she did the greatest thing in the world by giving birth to Maddie. We will always be thankful to her for bringing Maddie into the world. Maddie's birth mom wasn't ready to be a mommy and while she was praying to God for someone to help her, we were praying to God to bring us a baby because we really, really wanted to be a family. So God just answered everybody's prayers and Madison was adopted into our family. Now she is our daughter. And while our skin color is different, our hearts are exactly the same."

Jessica didn't even flinch at this explanation. She also wanted to know how we have two moms instead of a mom and a dad.

"Great question! There are all kinds of different families in the world. Some families, like yours, have just a mom. Some families have just a dad. Other kids are raised by their grandparents. And some families have two moms."

"Did you know my dad moved away because he and my mom are always fighting?" Jessica asked me. In a matter of seconds, her face crumpled and tears started sliding down her cheeks. "I really miss my dad."

I reached out and hugged this sad little girl as hard as I could. I held her in my arms until her breathing returned to normal. I assured her mother from a distance that everything was alright. Jessica went on to tell me little stories about her dad and how much she wants to see him again. I realized Jessica had questioned the design of Maddie's family because she was missing a piece of her own.

Before returning Jessica to her mother, I looked this little girl in the eye and promised her she could always talk to me about anything she wanted and I would always tell her the truth. I asked both girls to make nice with each other and they exchanged hugs before Jessica ran over to her mom. I picked up Maddie's dance bag where I had dropped it on the ground. I felt a little hand slide into mine and when I looked down at my firstborn, she smiled at me.

In a highly emotional situation, I remained calm. I modeled for my daughter the way to explain her family to other people and she was able to see that explanation received in a positive manner. I validated Madison's place in our family while at the same time uplifting her friend. I am still shocked at the success of the whole experience when I reflect on that Saturday morning a few years ago. Fortunately, no one needed to be dragged around back!

Consummating the adoption of each daughter did not automatically equip me with the answers to the hard questions in life. As my mother has always told me, there is no handbook to raising kids. Scripting the response to difficult situations requires study and practice. Oh yeah, and a lot of prayer, and possibly a good attorney's number on the speed dial of your cell phone just in case someone does get dragged around back.

Yes, I could have lashed out at this mother and child. I might have been totally justified in doing so but what would that have accomplished? I would have showed my daughter how to respond in anger and in doing so, encouraged her to do the same thing the next time this happens. I would have ruined the hard-earned friendship between Jessica's mother and me. I would have hurt a child's feelings. I would have locked myself into a state of anger, which serves absolutely no purpose.

For years, I have studied ways to respond to the hard questions and explored my feelings on the various components of race and adoption. In being an advocate for adoption, I have made a commitment to advocate for all children, regardless of how they came to be a member of their families. It would go against every fiber of my being to verbally assault a child. The only real choice, for me, was to respond in love. And thank God it worked. It could have gone another way, but it didn't.

Being a transracial family requires openness and tremendous love. Be open to new ideas, new concepts, and direction from within or from above, depending on your personal belief system. I am a Christian and my resource book for life reminds me how essential love is:

"Love is patient, love is kind. It does not envy, it does not boast, it is not proud. It is not rude, it is not self-seeking, it is not easily angered, it keeps no record of wrongs ... It always protects, always trusts, always hopes, always perseveres. Love never fails." — 1 Corinthians 13:4–8

I love my children with every cell in my body. I am profoundly thankful for each of them every day. They have changed my life in ways I could never have imagined. I want only the best for them and as I create opportunities for growth for my own children, I hope yours will benefit as well. I wish you peace for the journey and enough love to sustain the whole family.

# Acknowledgments

There are so many people who have impacted my life over the years and made this book possible. I have wanted to write a book since I was 15 years old and if I were to truly make a list of every person who influenced the writer in me, I would have to add many more pages in order to talk about Lyn Phillips, Lois Rodgers, Jennifer Doleac, Sarah Stanton, Nick Patras, Amy Randolph, Cameron Anderson; the list goes on and on. I truly believe I have been preparing for this moment my entire life. And I give God all thanks and praise for bringing me here. I am constantly amazed at what happens when I finally climb over the console to give God the wheel and just tag along for the ride.

To Kim — thank you for making me a mother. Thank you for opening my heart and my mind to the possibilities of fostering and adopting. Thank you for sharing this wild ride with me. You make it possible for me to follow my dreams and have a family at the same time. I love you.

To Madison, McKenzie, and Morgan — thank you for letting Mommy take the time to jot down some thoughts for other families just like ours. You continue to inspire me every day.

To Mom and Dad — thank you for your constant support. Mom you will always be my biggest fan and number one cheerleader. I don't know what I would do without your cheers! Dad, the older I get the more I realize how much I am like you. Thank you for showing how to work hard for the things I believe in. Thank you both for loving my children the way you do and thank you for loving me.

To my brother, Carl — I am a lucky, lucky girl to have such a great brother. It means the world to me that you love me just as I am.

To those parents who shared their experiences, strength and hope with the world — thank you Aimee Estep, Jennifer Danvers, Susan Griffith, Carol Boeck, Bobbie Kerr, Sandra Nosik, Pamela Jarvis, and Leah Ann O'Shieles.

To my writing buddies, Cheryl, Carolyn, and Tiffany — thank you for recognizing the writer in me! Thank you for your constant support and encouragement. Carolyn, you truly are the Book Whisperer! Cheryl, you have pushed me in such a loving way and believed in me for such a long time. Thank you. Tiffany, I couldn't ask for a better FON buddy. Your creativity is inspiring and I am honored to have your input on my project. Thank you.

To my dear friends, Julie and Evelyn — what would I do without you? Julie, you have been my best friend for 30 years now. Thank you for always believing in me and supporting whatever project I have ever undertaken. Ev, thank you for all the encouragement, support, and advice over such fabulous food at Dot's Place. I finally finished it!

To my Golden Girls — you may not always understand my ideas and may occasionally roll your eyes at my next project, but you always love me. And that goes a long way. Pat, It means the world to me that you love my stories of the girls so much. Thank you for reminding me what it feels like to be the middle child. Gail, I can never thank you enough for contributing to my love of books and obsession with words. To Kathy, I wish you could be here to see this. I know you will forever be watching over me.

To April, thank you for being my friend. I have learned more from you than you will ever know.

To Ruth and Ora — thank you for giving me a place to grow. The gift of your friendship is priceless.

To Parenting Across Color in Austin — thank you for letting me be one of you. Thank you for supporting me in good times and in bad.

To Jane – You are the greatest editor I could have hoped for! Thank you for making my dream and my words even better.

To Aimee — thank you for setting the ball in motion on this project. Without you in the beginning, I could have never crossed the finished line.

To COAC in Austin — thank you for helping me become the best parent I can be. We still have a long way to go and I sure am glad you're there!

To Dr. Stephen Terrell— thank you, Dr. Steve, for seeing what could be, long before I did.

To Kay Fowler and the Mt. Sinai Christian Academy Team — thank you for embracing my family and partnering with us to build a strong foundation in our children.

To Laurie B, the most patient photographer in the world who refused to quit until we got it right — thank you so much for capturing my beautiful family on film. I will treasure this photo long after the book is published.

To Ruby, Genevee, Martha, and the rest of the Region 7 CPS gang – thank you for the greatest opportunity of my life and thank you for your role in creating this family I adore. I realize yours is a thankless job with more heartbreak than most could bare, but I appreciate everything you do on behalf of kiddos everywhere.

To Karen Barry, perhaps the most creative person I know. Thank you for getting me and for understanding this project. I am forever in your debt.

# About Parenting Across Color

*Envisioning a world in which love has no color.*

Parenting Across Color (PAC) is dedicated to educating and supporting adoptive families comprised of white parents and black children, many of whom have spent time in the foster care system. Our goal is to assist families in raising strong, confident children who are comfortable in their own skin. To achieve this mission, PAC focuses on education, community building, adoption support, collaboration, and advocacy.

Parenting Across Color began as a local support group for adoptive families in Austin, Texas, in 2003. Created by Dr. Ruth McRoy and Ora Houston of St. James Episcopal Church, the group meets on a monthly basis to educate and support transracial families. Amy Ford took over as leader of the group in 2005, and in 2009, she organized the group into a nonprofit organization for the purpose of raising funds to support the needs of transracial families on a larger scale.

For more information or to learn how to start your own chapter of Parenting Across Color, visit the website at www.parentingacrosscolor.com.

Parenting Across Color

P.O. Box 5405

Round Rock, Texas, 78653

# About the Author

Amy Ford lives in Austin, Texas, with her partner, Kim, and their three daughters. Amy and Kim are founding members of their local chapter of Parenting Across Color (PAC). In December 2009, Amy organized the group to become a nonprofit to support and educate white parents who have adopted black children. She now serves as the Program Director for PAC. Amy also sits on the state board of the Council on Adoptable Children (COAC). A professional travel planner for 16 years, Amy now devotes her time to adoption advocacy, frequently leading workshops for transracial families.

# Resources

Here are a few personal recommendations for resources and products that I and other Parenting Across Color parents use on a regular basis.

## Books for Adults on Adoption and Transracial Parenting

*The Color of Water: A Black Man's Tribute to His White Mother*, by James McBride

*Life on the Color Line: The True Story of a White Boy Who Discovered He Was Black*, by Gregory Howard Williams

*I'm Chocolate, You're Vanilla: Raising Healthy Black and Bi-Racial Children in a Race Conscious World*, by Marguerite Wright.

*Inside Transracial Adoption*, by Beth Hall and Gail Steinberg

*Black Baby White Hands: A View from the Crib*, by Jaiya John

*Growing Up Black in White*, by Kevin Hofmann

*Loving Across the Color Line: A White Adoptive Mother Learns About Race*, by Sharon Rush

*In Their Own Voices: Transracial Adoptees Tell Their Stories*, by Rita J. Simon and Rhonda M. Roorda

*Weaving a Family: Untangling Race and Adoption*, by Barbara Katz Rothman

## Books for Adults on African-American Culture

*I Know Why the Caged Bird Sings*, by Maya Angelou

*The Bluest Eye*, by Toni Morrison

*1001 Things Everyone Should Know About African-American History*, by Jeffrey C. Stewart

*Why Are All the Black Kids Sitting Together in the Cafeteria?* by Beverly Daniel Tatum

The writings of Dr. Jawanza Kunjufu

## Books for Kids

*We Belong Together: A Book About Adoption and Families*, by Todd Parr

*I Like Myself!* by Karen Beaumont and David Catrow

*Skin Again*, by bell hooks and Chris Raschka

*Tell Me Again About the Night I Was Born*, by Jamie Lee Curtis and Laura Cornell
*I Love You Like Crazy Cakes*, by Rose A. Lewis and Jane Dyer
*Shades of Black*: *A Celebration of Our Children,* by Sandra L. Pinkney and Myles Pinkney
*I Love My Hair!* by Natasha Anastasia Tarpley and E.B. Lewis

## Books on Hair

*Hair Story: Untangling the Roots of Black Hair in America*, by Ayana Byrd and Lori Tharps
*Plaited Glory: For Colored Girls Who've Considered Braids, Locks, and Twists*, by Lonnice Brittenum Bonner
*It's All Good Hair: The Guide to Styling and Grooming Black Children's Hair*, by Michele N-K Collison
*Kinki Kreations: A Parent's Guide to Natural Black Hair Care for Kids*, by Jena Renee Williams
*I Love My Hair!* by Natasha Anastasia Tarpley and E.B. Lewis

## Hair Product Lines

Dudley's
Miss Jessie's Buttercream
Mixed Chicks
Humectress by Nexxus
Carol's Daughter

## Movies

*Crash*
*The Blindside*
*Places in the Heart*
*Fried Green Tomatoes*
*Good Hair*
*Soul Food*
*Beauty Shop*
*The Divine Secrets of the Ya-Ya Sisterhood*

## Magazines

*Adoptive Families*
*Parenting*

*Essence*
*Jet*
*Black Hair*

## Online Bookstores

Tapestry Books: www.tapestrybooks.com
Amazon: www.amazon.com

## Adoption Support and Resources

COAC (Council on Adoptable Children): www.coac.org
PAC (Parenting Across Color): www.parentingacrosscolor.com
NACAC (North American Council on Adoptable Children):
www.nacac.org
AKA (Adoption Knowledge Affiliates): www.adoptionknowledge.org
Pact: An Adoption Alliance, California: www.pactadopt.org
Evan B. Donaldson Adoption Institute: www.adoptioninstitute.org
Child Welfare Information Gateway: www.childwelfare.gov

## Famous Adoptive Parents

Alfre Woodard — actress
Angelina Jolie — actress
Barbara Walters — journalist
Ben Stein — actor and game show host
Burt Reynolds — actor
Calista Flockhart — actress
Connie Chung — news anchor
Diane Keaton — actress
Erma Bombeck — author
George Lucas — film director
Marie Osmond — singer
Michelle Pfeiffer — actress

## Famous Transracial Families

Angelina Jolie and Brad Pitt — daughter, Zahara, and sons, Maddox
and Pax
Sandra Bullock — son, Louis
Stephen Spielberg and Kate Capshaw — son, Theo, and daughter,
Mikaela

Tom Cruise — son, Connor
Michelle Pfeiffer — daughter, Claudia
Meg Ryan — daughter, Daisy
Madonna — son, David

# Endnotes

This section includes bibliographic information for sources referenced or reprinted in this book.

## Foreword

1. Adoption and Foster Care Analysis and Reporting System (AFCARS) FY 2008 (October 1, 2007 through September 30, 2008). U. S. Department of Health and Human Services, Administration for Children and Families, Administration on Children Youth and Families, Children's Bureau, (More information at www. Acf.hs.gov/programs/cb.)

## Chapter 1

1. Simon, R. J. and Alstein, H. (1977). *Transracial Adoption*, New York: John Wiley & Sons.

2. National Association of Black Social Workers, "Position Statement on Trans-Racial Adoption," September 1972. (Available online at the Adoption History Project website, www.uoregon.edu/~adoption/archive/NabswTRA.htm.)

3. The website of the National Association of Black Social Workers can be found at www.nabsw.org.

4. Kennedy, R. (1994). "Orphans of Separatism: The Painful Politics of Transracial Adoption," *The American Prospect*, Washington, D.C. (Available online at www.prospect.org.)

## Chapter 3

1. The University of Texas study referenced by Dr. Becky Bigler is: Pahlke, E.E. (2009). *European American Racial Socialization: The Influence of Mothers' Behaviors and Beliefs on Young Children's Racial Attitudes*, dissertation submitted to the University of Texas at Austin. Austin, Texas.

2. "Seven Common Transracial Parenting Mistakes," by Willie B. Garrett, first appeared in *Adoptive Parents* magazine, May/June 1999. Reprinted with permission of the author.

## Chapter 4

1. McRoy, R.G., & Zurcher, L.A. (1983). *Transracial and Inracial Adoptees: The Adolescent Years.* Springfield, Illinois: Charles C. Thomas. Second printing (1986).

2. Smith, S., McRoy, R., Freundlich, M., & Kroll, J. (2008). *Finding Families for African-American Children: The Role of Race and Law in Adoption from Foster Care.* New York, N.Y.: Evan B. Donaldson Adoption Institute. (This policy brief is available online at www.adoptioninstitute.org.)

**Chapter 7**

1. "A Transracially Adopted Child's Bill of Rights" is adapted by Liza Steinberg Triggs from "A Bill of Rights for Mixed Folks," by Marilyn Dramé and reprinted from *Inside Transracial Adoption*, by Beth Hall and Gail Steinberg of Pact: An Adoption Alliance. Reprinted with permission of the Pact: An Adoption Alliance. (Available online at www.pactadopt.org/press/articles/rights.html.)

**Chapter 8**

1. "Top 11 Critical Tools Needed to Style a Child's Hair," is reprinted from the workbook, *Pennsylvania Child Welfare Training Program 937-2: Hair and Skin Care for African-American and Bi-Racial Children*, written & created by Nicole Hewitt, MSW. Special contribution by Lori D. Hewitt, MS. Reprinted with permission of the author. (Available online at: www.pacwcbt.pitt.edu/.)

CPSIA information can be obtained at www.ICGtesting.com
Printed in the USA
BVOW070642300512

291354BV00003B/208/P